Cameo Glass

D1219399

ERRATA

p. 5, line 7, read "Blaszczyk" for "Blaszczk"

p. 5, para. 2, line 2, read "publication" for "publications"

p. 5, para. 2, line 8, read "Freiburg, Germany" for Freiborg, Germamy"

p. 23, caption for 4. Bottle, should read ". . . Turkey; last quarter of the 1st century B.C., first quarter of the 1st century A.D."

Credit line for catalog numbers 51, 65, 75, and 114 should read "Courtesy of Lillian Nassau and Leo Kaplan Antiques"

Credit line for catalog number 84 should read "Collection of Susan Kaplan"

Cameo Glass
Masterpieces from 2000 Years of Glassmaking
A special exhibition
The Corning Museum of Glass
Corning, New York
May 1 - October 31, 1982

Cover: The Portland Vase Disc. Rome, first half of 1st century A.D. Courtesy Trustees of The British Museum.

Back: The Moorish Bathers. England, 1898; signed George Woodall. Collection of Dr. and Mrs. Leonard S. Rakow.

Copyright © 1982
The Corning Museum of Glass
Corning, New York 14831

Printed in U.S.A.
Standard Book Number 0-87290-105-X
Library of Congress Catalog Card Number 82-70395

Art Direction: Anthony Russell
Design: Christopher Burg
Typography: Lettra Graphics, Inc.
Printing: Village Craftsmen
Photography: Raymond F. Errett and Nicholas L. Williams

This Exhibition is supported in part by a grant from the National Endowment for the Arts, in Washington, D.C., A Federal Agency.

We thank Pan American Airways, Inc., which generously underwrote transportation costs for many objects from Europe.

O
NK
5439
.J33
G6
1982

DABNEY LANCASTER LIBRARY
LONGWOOD COLLEGE
FARMVILLE, VIRGINIA 23901

Contents

82-11401

Foreword

*I*n the 19th century, a demand for ornate household furnishings "in the latest taste" stimulated a revival and rejuvenation of many earlier styles. Many householders wanted a "Turkish" corner or a "Gothic" music room where they could relax and contemplate their good fortune amid richly colored, elaborately worked surroundings which reflected their good taste. Among the popular styles in the period, "classical" was a return to the time-tested forms of ancient Greece and Rome. In glass, this interest resulted in the duplication of one of the world's most famous ancient objects, the Portland Vase, a first century A.D. Roman cameo glass vessel. The response to the completion and display of this masterpiece was extraordinary. It marked the beginning of a fashion for cameo glass which would endure for nearly fifty years.

For the purposes of this catalog, the term "cameo glass" is used to refer only to cased glass objects with two or more differently colored layers. The outer layer is usually an opaque or opalescent white, and the outer layer or layers have been carved to leave the decoration standing in relief against a body of contrasting color. Shading is produced by thinning down the carved layer; highlights are created where the glass is left thickest.

It is appropriate that many of the Woodall pieces in this catalog are inscribed "Gem Cameo." They are indeed gems of glassmaking and that is the way in which they should be displayed and regarded. These glassmaking masterpieces, extraordinarily delicate in detail, bold in color, and elegant in restrained form, can justly hold their place among the world's costliest treasures.

Both this catalog and the exhibition it records document the 2000-year cameo glass tradition. The objects shown are the best of their kind, be they ancient, Islamic, Chinese, or English. This exhibition is the beneficiary of the willingness of the owners of the treasures shown here to lend them to us temporarily. No museum can ever hope for any stronger expression of support. We are truly grateful.

Dwight P. Lanmon, Director
The Corning Museum of Glass

Acknowledgments

The plans for *Cameo Glass, Masterpieces from 2000 Years of Glassmaking* began in 1979, but the exhibition would never have occurred in 1982 without worldwide cooperation. Many European and American colleagues have provided information, photographs, and objects to help make this extraordinary visual feast possible. The constant and keen interest of Leonard and Juliette Rakow during the planning stages of the exhibition and their contributions to this catalog were vital. Their generosity in sharing their unparalleled collection with the public and gradually transferring it to The Corning Museum of Glass is acknowledged with our deepest gratitutde. It is the intent of the catalog to discuss and illustrate the many glorious objects fashioned in the cameo glass technique, some of which have never been seen or published before. We would like to thank the following institutions and collectors who have generously lent objects to this exhibition from their collections:

Dr. and Mrs. Ronald Berg
Dr. and Mrs. Henry Blount
The British Museum, London
Broadfield House Glass Museum, Dudley, England
The Chrysler Museum, Norfolk, Virginia
City of Bristol Museum and Art Gallery, Bristol, England
The Corning Museum of Glass
The Currier Gallery of Art, Manchester, New Hampshire
Carl U. Fauster
Mr. and Mrs. Billy Hitt
Leo Kaplan Antiques
Susan Kaplan
Kofler-Truniger Collection
Kunsthistorisches Museum, Vienna
L.A. Mayer Memorial Institute for Islamic Art, Jerusalem
Marian Swayze Mayer
The Metropolitan Museum of Art, New York
Musée des Beaux-Arts et d'Archéologie, Besançon, France
Museum of Fine Arts, Boston
Museum zu Allerheiligen, Schaffhausen, Switzerland
Dr. and Mrs. Peter H. Plesch
Dr. and Mrs. Leonard S. Rakow
Horace E. Richardson
Drs. Jerome and Arline Rosen
Royal Brierley Crystal, Brierley Hill, England
Smithsonian Institution, The National Museum of American Art and
The National Museum of American History
Mr. and Mrs. Bernard Starr
The Toledo Museum of Art
Yale University Art Gallery, New Haven, Connecticut

For the assistance from friends and colleagues, I wish to acknowledge Brian Cook, J. Michael Rogers, Hugh Tait, and Veronica Tatton-Brown, The British Museum; Nancy Merrill, Chrysler Museum; Nicholas Thomas and Peter Hardie, City of Bristol Museum; Charles Hajdamach, Broadfield House Glass Museum, Dudley; Philip Zimmerman, Currier Gallery of Art; Stan Evison and

Eric Stott, Dema Glass, Amblecote, England; Wolfgang Oberleitner, Kunsthistorisches Museum, Vienna; Philip Lagrange, Musée des Beaux-Arts et d'Archéologie, Besançon; Gabriel Moriah and Rachel Hasson, L.A. Mayer Memorial for Islamic Art; Dietrich von Bothmer and Joan Mertens, The Metropolitan Museum of Art; Edward Brovarski and James Watt, Museum of Fine Arts, Boston; Max Freivogel, Museum zu Allerheiligen, Schaffhausen; Harry Lowe, Susan Myers, Regina Blaszczk, and the late Joshua Taylor, National Museum of American Art; Colonel Reginald Silvers Williams-Thomas and Sam Thompson, Royal Brierley Crystal; Roger Mandel, Kurt Luckner, Patricia Whitesides, The Toledo Museum of Art; John Malett, Victoria and Albert Museum, London; Susan Matheson, Yale University Art Gallery.

Many hours were spent by others who tracked objects, documented facts, or supplied photographs for study or publications. We hope we do not overlook anyone when we thank:
Claude Bensimon, St. Maure, France; Yvonne Brunhammer, Paris; Jean-Pierre Catry, Paris; Max Erlacher, Corning; Leonard Gorelick, Littleneck, New York; Leo, Allen, and Susan Kaplan, New York; Brigitte Klesse, Cologne, Germany; Gawain MacKinley, New York; Kenneth Northwood, South Devon, England; Gunter Puhze, Freiborg, Germamy; Christopher Sheppard, London; Herbert Woodward, Dudley; Fausto Zevi, Naples, Italy.

Among our own staff at The Corning Museum of Glass, I would like to thank Robert Brill for his many observations about ancient technology; Thomas Buechner, Priscilla Price, and Joseph Maio for the design, organization, and installation of the exhibition. Phyllis Casterline, Charleen Edwards, Dwight Lanmon, John Martin, and Louise Volpe deserve special thanks for helping ready this manuscript and making welcome editorial suggestions. Photography for both the catalog and exhibition was done by Raymond Errett and Nicholas Williams.

Sidney M. Goldstein
Chief Curator
The Corning Museum of Glass

The word "cameo" often evokes the image of an oval pin with raised, classical figures on a dark background, worn by a grandmother or favorite aunt. That treasured cameo brooch, probably carved from a piece of shell, was a magnet for small hands, a fascinating glimpse of the classical past, a cherished family keepsake bequeathed from one generation to the next.

Man has produced such delicately shaded carvings for thousands of years by working the colored shell layers. As early as 3rd century B.C., Hellenistic craftsmen were creating large cameo plaques of layered, semi-precious stones for imperial gifts; it fell to the Roman glassmaker and lapidary to refine this art to its ultimate by producing some of the most luxurious vessels in the world.

Consider the complexity of the glassmaker's task: after the invention of glassblowing in the middle of the 1st century B.C., glassmakers learned to cover or "case" a gather of glass of one color with a second layer in a contrasting color. The resulting *blank* could then be given to a lapidary for cutting and carving. The technical problems were overwhelming, for a piece could shatter at the slightest miscalculation. Objects often took years to produce; some were made with as many as seven layers. The finished cameo carving, usually with a meticulously-cut scene in relief, became the valued possession of the wealthy patrons who could afford such expensive luxuries. What vessel could match the delicate carving of such a brittle material? Who could fail to note and appreciate the details of gesture, of hair, of expression, of musculature which made each cameo a masterpiece in a most difficult medium? Cost was obviously no deterrent. Consider, for example, the famous Portland Vase. Now in The British Museum, it is not only one of the masterpieces of ancient artistry but also of ancient cameo glass. Made in the early 1st century A.D., its depths, its subtleties, its design and proportions combined to make it the most famous piece of ancient glass in existence.

Empires rose and fell; glassmaking traditions sometimes faltered or were modified. After the fall of the Roman Empire, the cameo glass tradition was lost in the West but continued in the centers of Islamic glassmaking (7th–15th centuries). Although the style was quite different, the technique was the same. Islamic patrons preferred their cameo-carved reliefs on colorless glass to imitate rock crystal, not the more familiar white-on-blue glass carving which was typical of Roman cameo glass.

In China, glass was never valued as highly as in the West either for objects of daily use or luxury. Nevertheless, glassmaking attracted imperial interest in the 17th and 18th centuries under the supervision of European Jesuits at the court. Glass cameo carving in China evidently began some time in the early 18th century and may have been influenced directly by earlier ties in previous centuries during trade with the Islamic world. We do not know whether the cameo technique was rediscovered in the 18th century or whether it resulted from an attempt to imitate carved jade. The Chinese style and color combinations were in marked contrast to Greek, Roman, or Islamic cameo glass carving. A red-on-white color combination was not the only cameo glass produced; other combinations were strange, if not shocking, to Western eyes. As one would expect, the vessel shapes and functions were quite different from typical Western forms.

In the 19th century, the Portland Vase became the benchmark against which the standard of "Beauty is truth, truth beauty" was matched. There were many replicas of the vase in other materials, but none in glass. Josiah Wedgwood had produced his famous black and white "jasperware" ceramic copy made from an actual cast of the ancient vase in the 18th century. When a classical revival swept England in the 19th century, a challenge was issued to any glass engraver who could accurately reproduce the Portland Vase. John Northwood (1836–1902), already an accomplished glass engraver, worked from 1873 to 1876 to reproduce the famous piece. Though his copy cracked before it was finished, it was repaired, exhibited, and he was awarded the £1000 prize.

The public acclaim was enormous! Demand for cameo glass increased, and English glasshouses rushed to supply the market. The laborious process of making the costly decorated figural pieces meant that the production could not begin to satisfy the demand for cameo glass. Therefore, less elaborate objects were produced, and cost-cutting techniques were used to produce simple acid-etched pieces with little or no hand carving. The fashion flourished until the early 20th century when rising production costs, cheap imitations, and changing tastes caused its demise. The fascination for cameo glass of all periods, however, remains, and today a few glassmakers are attempting still another revival.

S.M.G.

As the Hellenistic empires of the third century B.C. were systematically conquered and often ruthlessly plundered, Republican Rome quickly became the focal point of wealth and patronage of the arts. Even if the accounts of ancient historians such as Pliny and Livy are grossly exaggerated, the quantities of artwork and precious metals brought to Rome must have been staggering.

Pliny, a historian of simple tastes, recalls that luxury items from the continent of Asia were first sent to Italy when Scipio brought more than 1,400 pounds of engraved silverware and 1,500 pounds of gold vases in 189 B.C. He laments that Rome learned not just to admire foreign opulence but to love it![1] Such opulence was hardly a desirable attribute of a Republican form of government.

By the first century B.C., this massive amount of foreign art and culture was being absorbed and disseminated. Pearls and gems excited interest, but Pliny was less than enthusiastic when a gaming table three feet by four feet, made from two gemstones, as well as dozens of pearl crowns, and a pearl portrait of Pompey himself were flaunted at Pompey's triumph celebrating his Asiatic victories in 61 B.C.[2]

Descriptions of such wealth leave little doubt that many Roman patrons could easily afford the costliest carved gemstones. Indeed the quality of gem carving, both relief and intaglio (cutting the design into the surface), showed a marked improvement as the Republic faded and the Peace of Augustus heralded a new era for the Roman people. Augustus himself commissioned one of the most famous gem carvers, Dioskourides, to create his seal.[3] In his passion for gem carving, Augustus was not a leader but followed a tradition encouraged by such predecessors as the dictator Sulla[4] and Julius Caesar.[5] Other wealthy Romans acquired a taste for owning personal seals, and craftsmen flocked to Rome seeking patrons: "Every Roman with any pretention to dignity had his own seal . . . the concentration of wealth to Rome in this age attracted Greek and Oriental artisans to the capital."[6]

The sophistication of the great gems carved in the cameo tradition is impressive. These huge stone cameos, such as the *Gemma Augustea* (Fig. 1)[7] or the *Grande Camée de France*,[8] imperial commissions as large as dinner plates, exemplify the technical skill and virtuosity that can be seen in Augustan art both on the official and secular level. The crisp quality of stone carving on the famous *Ara Pacis*,[9] the casting and finishing of vegetal design on the silver vessels from Boscoreale[10] or Hildesheim,[11] and the carving on the *Gemma Augustea* reflect the popular style.

Each shows the acquired taste for earlier Greek art, a Hellenistic neo-classicism which was executed by the most adept imported craftsmen. Attention to detail was paramount, composition was often purely decorative, and the infusion of historical and political propaganda on several levels was typically Roman. The scene

1. Pliny, *Natural History*, 33, 148-50. 2. *Ibid.*, 37, 12-14. 3. *Ibid.*, 37, 8. 4. *Ibid.*, 37, 9.
5. Suetonius, *The Divine Julius*, 47.
6. Donald Earl, *The Age of Augustus*, New York: Crown Publishers, Inc., 1968, p. 131.
7. Ranuccio Bianchi Bandinelli, *Rome: The Center of Power 500 B.C. to A.D. 200* (trans. by Peter Green) New York: G. Braziller, 1970, p. 194ff, figs. 209-210 for both cameos; *CAH* IV, p. 156; George M.A. Hanfmann, *Roman Art*, Greenwich, Conn: New York Graphic Society, 1964, p. 249, colorplate 17; Heinz Kahler, *The Art of Rome and Her Empire*, New York: Crown Publishers, Inc., 1965, p. 71, colorplate on p. 75; Simon, *Portlandvase* p. 50, pl. 12. F. Eichler and E. Kris, *Die Kameen Im Kunsthistorischen Museum*, Publikationen aus der Kunsthistorischen Sammlungen in Wien, Band II, Vienna, 1927, pp. 9, 52-56, no. 7, pl.4.
8. H. Jucker, "Der Grosse Pariser Kameo," *JDAI* 91, 1976, pp. 211-250 for bibliography. Marilyn Brown, "Ingres, Gautier, and the Ideology of The Cameo Style of the Second Empire," *Arts Magazine* 56, no. 4, 1981, pp. 94-99,

Fig. 1 *Gemma Augustea*, banded Arabian onyx, Roman, about 10-20 A.D., Kunsthistorisches Museum, Vienna, photo Kunsthistorisches Museum, Vienna.

on the cameo fragment in the Kunsthistorisches Museum (No. 1) seems to be relatively straightforward: the Emperor Augustus seated beside the personification of Rome. The composition of this fragment is similar to that of the *Gemma Augustea* or the *Grande Camée de France*. Yet, on both of these works, scholars argue that more than one event may be represented and that several *levels* of interpretation are reasonable (historical, allegorical, or mythological); there is not even general agreement as to the identification of the figures.

Amid the opulence of Augustan Rome, glass technology provided lapidaries with a new medium on which to continue this carved tradition. The discovery of glass-blowing enabled glassmakers to case layers of one color over another.[12] Form and color were no longer *discovered and adapted* as the gem carver worked a natural stone, for he knew exactly how the various color bands in the glass blank would relate to each other and to the general vessel shape. Surprisingly, they were not affected by the problems of glass incompatibility which plagued their Victorian

fig. 2, primarily concerned with the development of painting styles; the *Grand Camée de France* is featured in this article with useful bibliography.

9. Ernest Nash, *Pictorial Dictionary of Ancient Rome*, Vol. I, New York: Praeger, (2nd ed. rev.) 1968, pp. 63-73. Erika Simon, *Ara Pacis Augustae*, Greenwich, Conn: New York Graphic Society, (n.d.), good photographic documentation and bibliography.

10. A. Oliver, Jr., *Silver for the Gods, 800 Years of Greek and Roman Silver*, Toledo: Toledo Museum of Art, 1977, p. 137, no. 87, 88; D.E. Strong, *Greek and Roman Gold and Silver Plate*, Ithaca: Cornell University, 1966, pp. 125ff.

11. Oliver, *op. cit.*, p. 126, no. 80 and p. 130, no. 83; Ulrich Gehrig, *Hildesheimer Silberfund*, Berlin: Brüder Hartmann 1967; Strong, *op. cit.*, p. 127ff.

12. Evidence for the discovery and widespread use of glassblowing in the mid-1st century B.C. is presented most comprehensively to date in David Grose, "Early Blown Glass: The Western Evidence,"*JGS* 19, 1977, pp. 9-29.

successors.[13] The cased blank was carefully annealed by the *vitriarius*[14] (the man who worked with the hot glass). Not only were hollow cameo-carved vessels now possible (they were nearly *impossible* to create from banded stones), but also the irregularities left to nature in any layered gemstone were entirely eliminated. It would seem logical that the gem cutter ordered a glass vessel of the desired shape and color sequence, each layer being of a specified thickness, to give the desired effect.

Just how this casing was accomplished is still unclear. Several techniques may have been used to apply a contrasting glass layer over the gather on a blow-pipe. The following ways may have been employed:

1. Dipping, the most obvious, is used today for glasses which have a single casing.[15] When a gather of blue glass is dipped into a pot of hot opaque white glass, the end or bottom of the gather tends to accumulate more white glass than the sides. The excess is removed by tooling and shearing. This operation requires a great deal of control; otherwise the glassworker is not able to maintain the uniform thickness of the outer layer.

2. Preformed cups or cylinders are also used today in casing glasses. Their use has been mentioned as an alternate possibility for the formation of the Portland Vase blank,[16] and this technique was certainly known in the 19th century when glass-makers were trying to duplicate the Portland. Making a two-color blank by this technique is not difficult, but it is hard to envision how a five or a six-layer cameo (No. 8) would be cased this way.

3. Several authors refer to blowing the form and casing it.[17] The problem with this technique is one of marvering the outer surface without distorting the blown shape.

Study of many fragments suggests that the two layers were very well-marvered and frequently reheated to insure as much contact along the interface as possible.[18] Such manipulation and repeated marvering would be difficult if the blue gather were very much inflated or shaped to the finished specified form. Thus it would seem easier to wind on the casing glass over a paraison or solid gather.

4. In an unpublished manuscript on cameo glass, Fahim Kouchakji mentioned the technique of applying trails to the surface of the glass.[19] Although he alludes to this process in his later publication with Gustavus Eisen, he expands on an elaborate molding process which is very difficult to reconstruct.[20] Nevertheless, winding on softened trails or possibly strips of glass would be one way to insure an even

13. Robert Brill, Research Scientist of The Corning Museum of Glass has pointed out that chemical analyses of the Roman dark blue transparent glasses and white opaque glasses indicate that their coefficients of expansion are very close to one another and that consequently the glasses were entirely compatible. This has been verified by actual laboratory determinations of the coefficients of expansion for several Roman glasses including the dark blue and white opaque glasses from the unfinished cameo glass in the Higgins Armory referred to above (Fig. 2).
14. W.A. Thorpe, "The Prelude to European Cut Glass," *J. Soc. Glass Tech.* 22, Trans., 1938, p. 20. Trowbridge, *Philological Studies*, p. 66.
15. Haynes, p. 21.
16. Apsley Pellatt, *Curiosities of Glass Making*, London, 1849, pp. 114-116.
17. Harden, "Ancient Glass, II: Roman," footnote 19 ". . . probably made by blowing the blue inner layer and then gathering the white around it. Alternatively the inner layer might have been blown into the outer one, but this seems far less likely in this instance."; Simon, *Portlandvase*, p. 3. "Ob er durch Blasen gewonnenist oder durch Herausschleifen aus Einem glasblock, Kann bis heute nicht mit Sickerheit gesagt werden . . .", cutting from a solid block seems extremely unlikely; Goldstein, *Pre-Roman*, p. 33.
18 The interface of the blue and white layers is consistently well bonded. Although the depth of field for this edge examination was limited, no pockets or gaps were noted along the clean edges or within the focusing range. Numerous seed bubbles and slightly larger bubbles were noted, all of which were spherical, not deformed. Some small bubbles formed at the interface; these too were perfectly spherical, each having deformed the softened glass above and below the interface.
19. Fahim Kouchakji, Cameo manuscript. [Photostatic copy of typescript, n.d., 1920s] Confidential.
20. G. A. Eisen assisted by F. Kouchakji, *Glass*, New York: William E. Rudge, 1927, p. 155; he suggests the design was cut into a mold, and white glass pads were pressed into this and thinned. Cylinders of dark glass were

distribution of one layer over the base glass.

Inflation would further reduce the thickness of the final casing. The technique would be related to the core-forming process where glass was gathered over a core by winding on hot glass from the furnace.[21] Marvering and reheating would press and flatten the glass against the rigid substructure.[22] The popular Venetian tradition of casing glass by picking up flattened strips of glass from the marvering table may have evolved as a variation of this technique

5. Finally, one must consider a technique which is used by contemporary glassmakers but which may be of considerable antiquity. The process involves blowing a gather of the outer white layer into a large bubble and pushing the blue paraison deeply into it. The casing bubble is then sheared, and the cased blank reheated.[23] It is a difficult process which often results in uneven fusion along the interface if it is not done correctly.

Fig. 2 Unfinished cameo glass fragment, Roman, early 1st century A.D., John Woodman Higgins Armory, Worcester, Mass.

Some of these explanations are hypothetical; the Roman methods remain unknown. We cannot confidently point to any single technique and confirm that it was used in antiquity. The basic glassblowing tools and processes have changed very little in the past 2,000 years and we should not assume an extraordinarily complex technology for the manufacture of cameo blanks. Future research may help clarify this vexing problem.

*H*aving failed to give a clear answer to the question of forming the glass blank, let us move from the skills of the *vitriarius* to those of the *diatretarius*[24], the cutter or engraver of Roman glass, especially cameo vessels. Stylistically and technically it seems reasonable that the artists and craftsmen who carved natural gemstones into imperial cameos were the same individuals who worked in glass. Stones such as agate, sardonyx, and chalcedony were softer than glass, but quartz and obsidian were somewhat harder. The cutting, faceting, grinding, polishing, and carving of stone as hard or harder than glass was commonly and continuously practiced in antiquity using various tools.[25] Throughout history lapidaries were using a variety of tools fed with abrasive powders to cut and polish stones. According to Pliny, there was a wide range of abrasives available to the Roman gem carver.[26] Some 1,500 years before man ever made glass, Egyptian craftsmen were fashioning objects from granite, basalt, diorite, flint, obsidian, or quartz.[27]

By the third century B.C. the ancient bow drill had been adapted and mounted into a horizontal position to form a simple lathe.[28] The often-cited tombstone of

fused in the mold to form the body, and the whole exterior surface was finished with a carving tool. This "pseudo-*pâte de verre*" technique is not substantiated by the examination of Roman cameo glass fragments.

21. Goldstein, *Pre-Roman*, p. 27

22. There is some uncertainty about the line created at the interface. At the crossection of a trail-decorated fragment of a typical core-formed glass, there is usually a scalloped interface where the trails have pressed into the softened outer surface of the vessel. Unlike core-formed vessels, if trails were closely wound on to case the glass, they would touch each other and tend to flatten out rather than displace the glass beneath. One should be able to see some type of regular bubble pattern following the trail flow, but none has been observed on the cameo fragments which have been examined.

23. I am indebted to Max Roland Erlacher, Corning, New York, a master engraver, for discussing this technique. Erlacher, who has been copper-wheel engraving for over 30 years, has recently begun to carve cameo glass.

24. Trowbridge, *Philological Studies*, p. 119; Thorpe, *op. cit.*, p. 20.

25. A recent symposium organized by Leonard Gorelick and A. John Gwinnett focused on the art of the lapidary from early paleolithic tool fabrication through the incredible complexities of gem cutting in the Islamic world. The symposium papers are published in *Expedition* 23, no. 4 and 24, no. 1, 1981.

26. Pliny, *N.H.*, 36, 9-10.

27. In his monumental work on Egyptian technology, Lucas summarizes the work of previous authors on the fabrication of stone vessels. A. Lucas, *Ancient Egyptian Materials and Industries*, (4th Ed., rev. and enlarged by J.R. Harris), London: Edward Arnold, 1962, pp. 72-74, 421-423.

28. Illustrations of the bow drill exist in tomb reliefs from the middle of the third millennium B.C. while the actual wooden tools are preserved from tombs of the 2nd millennium B.C.; L. Gorelick and A. J. Gwinnett, "The Origin and Development of the Ancient Near Eastern Cylinder Seal," *Expedition* 23, no. 4, 1981, pp. 23-25, fig. 9.

the Hellenistic gem-engraver, Douris of Sardis, depicts the lathe;[29] some writers feel that lathes existed as early as the 3rd millennium B.C.[30]

The cutting and engraving of Roman glass was certainly accomplished with a rotary instrument which powered abrasive-fed wheels; it is probable that the instrument might well have been an "all-purpose" tool which could be adapted as a lathe or engraving wheel as needed.[31]

A fist-sized fragment of cameo glass (Fig. 2), in the John Woodman Higgins Armory confirms that a cutting wheel was used in the Roman tradition.[32] The piece must have formed the central portion of a large plaque or plate not unlike the plaques or plates (Nos. 12-15) in the catalog. The design of a central boss with radiating flutes or grooves was being cut into the thick white casing layer when it probably broke. The grooves are wide and deep with rounded and tapering ends characteristic of wheel-cut strokes.

Examination of many cameo vessels and fragments confirms that an engraving wheel was certainly used to fashion some of the more delicate designs. The treat-

ment of the drapery and the lines delineating the fingers of the woman on the Morgan cup (Fig. 3, No. 3) are typical of wheel-engraving.

However, engraving wheels were certainly not the only cutting tools used by the Roman cameo-carver. Evidence of the use of hand tools for cutting, scraping, and polishing is clearly evident. Perhaps they were as simple as those used by their 19th-century successors (Nos. 155, 156). The tufts of hair on the satyr's head from the skyphos in the exhibition (Fig. 4, No. 16) seem to have been finished with hand tools, not a wheel. Much of the final polishing and modeling of figures seems to have been accomplished with a non-rotary tool.

In the final analysis, one must marvel at the quality of detail achieved by the Roman cameo carver even though it does not equal the technical excellence achieved by George Woodall in the late 19th and early 20th century.[33] One needs the assistance of a microscope to study the carved details on these ancient vessels. For the perennial question of *how did they do it without a magnifying glass?* the reader is referred to an intriguing suggestion that such craftsmen were myopic and thus had unusually close vision![34]

Fig. 3 Woman at the shrine of Dionysos; detail, *The Morgan Cup*, No. 3.

Knowing the Augustan delight in obscure Neoclassical motifs and the Roman sense of order and history, a discussion of style and figural representation is inappropriate (if not impossible) in this brief introductory catalog.

29. R. J. Charleston, "Wheel-Engraving and Cutting: Some Early Equipment. I. Engraving," *JGS* 6, 1964, p. 86, fig. 2.
30. Gorelick and Gwinnett, *op. cit.*, pp. 24-25; Goldstein, "A Unique Royal Head," *JGS* 21, 1979, p. 12; Goldstein, "Pre-Roman and Persian Glass: Some Observations on Objects in The Corning Museum of Glass," D. Schmandt-Besserat (ed.), *Ancient Persia: The Art of an Empire*, Malibu: Undena Publications 1980, pp. 47-50; Martin Robertson, *A History of Greek Art*, Cambridge: Cambridge University Press, 1975, p. 148; Charleston, *op. cit.*, p. 86; V. Gordon Ghilde, "Rotary Motion," p. 193, footnote 1, in C. Singer *et al.*, *A History of Technology* I, New York: Oxford University Press, 1954.
31. Charleston, *op. cit.*, p. 87.
32. S. M. Goldstein, *A Catalogue of Ancient Glass in the John Woodman Higgins Armory*, (n.p.) 1969, p. 7, no. 26; the base glass is 2.5 cm thick and the white casting is 1.5 cm thick; formerly Metropolitan Museum, *Greau Cat.* p. 220, no. 1620.
33. See p. 56 figs. 28-29 for enlarged areas which show extraordinary detail of Woodall's carved design.
34. L. Gorelick and A. J. Gwinnett, "Close Work Without Magnifying Lenses?" *Expedition* 23, no. 2, 1981, pp. 27-34; "Close Work without Magnifying Lenses? Discussion of suggestions from readers of Expedition," *Expedition* 23, no. 4, pp. 15-16.

The interpretation of the decoration on the Portland Vase (Fig. 5) continues to occupy scholars after more than three centuries; it is unlikely that any superficial discussion here would add to our knowledge.[35] The myth of Peleus and Thetis is the most widely accepted interpretation.

None of the cameo vessels other than the Portland Vase seems to depict a scene of comparable complexity. Most, however, deal with Dionysian rites and the revelation of some secret mystery. Several of these cameo glasses (Nos. 3, 5, 17) form the rough chronology for the Roman portion of the present exhibition.[36] Most cameo scenes present some sort of sacrifice or initiation, even those with clearly Egyptian-style motifs such as the Kofler-Truniger bottle (No. 4) or the Corning fragment (No. 9). The scene on the bottle is an Egyptian sacrifice; the Corning fragment is decorated with two men bearing gifts or offerings. Many fragments in museum collections are decorated with grape vine or leaf motifs. Many of these same fragments preserve the profile of a cup, or more specifically, the handle or profile of a skyphos, a favorite wine vessel made both in glass and metal. One exception to the Dionysiac-related decorative cycles is the scene of two chariots with drivers (Fig. 6) recently advertised on the European market.[37] The faces under the handles are said to be youths, not satyrs or Dionsyiac masks. Since the vessel is a skyphos, perhaps this scene can be explained as a chariot race during the Dionysiac games.

Fig. 4 Satyr with sirynx; detail, *Parthian Skyphos*, No. 16.

We hope that one of the more useful elements of this catalog for those with an interest in ancient cameo glass will be an updated list of major objects and their present location.[38] Some known pieces must be deleted and new objects have been added. Excluding fragments, the extant Roman cameo glasses are;

1. The Portland Vase, The British Museum. This vessel (Fig. 5) is the most important and unquestionably the most beautifully executed cameo glass preserved today.[39]

2. The Naples Vase, Museo Archeologico, Naples. This vessel (Fig. 7) is more heavily carved than the Portland Vase, but the carving is not so carefully executed; the style is more robust.[40]

3. The Morgan Cup, The Corning Museum of Glass, Corning, New York. This small cup (No. 3) is one of only two preserved cameo vessels which has not been broken and repaired.

4. The Parthian Skyphos, private collection. This vessel (No. 16) is said to have been found in a Parthian tomb in Iran. It is the most important early cameo vessel

---

35. In addition to the extensive bibliographical references provided by Simon, *Portlandvase*, and Haynes in their respective monographs, there are two recent reconsiderations of the Portland. Evelyn Harrison has had some additional thoughts on the scenes; E. B. Harrison, "The Portland Vase: Thinking It Over" in *Essays in Memoriam Otto Brendel*, Mainz, 1976, pp. 131-142; John Hind has most recently suggested the vase as an "imperial essay in adapting Hellenic legend to relate to Rome's past . . . and Augustan present,"; Hind, "Greek and Roman Epic Scenes on the Portland Vase," *JGS* 99, 1979, pp. 20-25; Geoffrey Wills, "Sir William Hamilton and the Portland Vase," *Apollo*, September 1979, pp. 195-201. Leonard S. and Juliette Rakow, "The Glass Replicas of the Portland Vase," *JGS* 24, 1982 (in press).

36. Simon, *JGS* 6, pp. 13-30.

37. See p. 15, No. 12.

38. Simon *JGS* 6, pp. 13-30; Simon, *Portlandvase*; Kisa, pp. 578-590; Eisen, pp. 155-167.

39. See footnote 35; also No. 5 in this catalog.

40. H. 30 cm, found in 1834 in Pompeii. Haynes, pp. 23-24, pl. 12; Eisen, p. 157, pls. 19-20; Kisa, 582, pls. 8, 9, also early bibliography; the Naples Vase is frequently illustrated. C. Isings, *Antiek Glas*, Amsterdam: J.H. DeBussy, 1965, p. 23, pl. 8, for the infrequently published side showing putti crushing grapes.

Fig. 5 *The Portland Vase*, Roman, early 1st century A.D., The British Museum, photo courtesy The Trustees of the British Museum.

which has to come to light in the last quarter century. It is said to be one of a pair. If so, a fourteenth piece of cameo glass must be added to the list.

5. *The Torrita Vase*, Archaeological Museum, Florence. This vessel (Fig. 8) was found in Etruria and is stylistically close to the Portland Vase.[41]

6. Jug or pitcher, Musée des Beaux Arts, Besançon, France. This jug (No. 17), found in a Gallo-Roman cemetery, was probably a local product.

7. *The Auldjo Jug*, The British Museum. A fragmentary vessel (No. 6), decorated with vine leaves and grapes.

8. Bottle, Kofler-Truniger Collection, Lucerne. The small vessel (No. 4) is decorated with an Egyptian-style offering scene.

9. Trulla, Museo Nazionale, Naples. This vessel (Fig. 9) was used as a dipper to transfer wine from a *krater* or bowl to a drinking vessel.[42] The central design on the interior is a satyr head surrounded by a garland of grape leaves.

10, 11. Plaques, Museo Nazionale, Naples. These two plaques (Figs. 10, 11) are virtually complete and are among the important figural scenes in the cameo technique to be preserved.[43]

12. Chariot Skyphos, Private Collection. This drinking vessel (Fig. 6) is decorated with two racing chariots.[44]

13. Hunting Bowl, Museum zu Allerheiligen, Schaffhausen, Switzerland. The bowl (No. 18) is a 4th-century Roman masterpiece carved in the cameo tradition and the most recently discovered.

Fig. 6 **Skyphos with charioteers, Roman, 1st century A.D., private collection. Photo** *Weltkunst.*

T he list of extant cameo vessels numbers just over a dozen. A few objects which have been cited in the literature as being of Roman date are not included since they were probably produced in Venice. This interesting group of vessels was made in the late 19th and early 20th centuries and decorated by acid-etching as the wave of Neoclassical revival crested in the Italian glass factories.[45] Representative pieces in American collections have been included in the exhibition so that students and scholars may compare the style and surface treatment of these vessels to their ancient counterparts. These objects differ from Roman cameo both in subject matter and profile. The decorations are usually isolated figures which were derived from either Roman marble reliefs[46] or molded glass plaques.[47]

Among this Venetian group, the Moore cameo vase in the Yale University Art Gallery (No. 87) and the Curtis Vase in The Toledo Museum of Art (No. 89) have been incorrectly cited as being ancient.[48] Eisen also illustrates a cameo alabastron in the Bibliothèque Nationale, Paris, which relates to this group.[49] In addition to these three *historicizing* Venetian cameos, one should include the vases in the

41. Simon, *JGS* 6, pp. 21-24, figs. 9-13 for bibliography and discussion.

42. Simon, *Portlandvase*, p. 47, pl. 24, 1. The museum was unable to supply a photograph of this piece probably because of the disruptions caused by the earthquake in 1981. A photograph from The Corning Museum Archives is reproduced here: we apologize for the poor quality.

43. Dr. Fausto Zevi, Soprintendenza, kindly provided photographs of objects in the Museo Nazionale, Naples.

44. *Weltkunst* 46, no. 20, 15 October 1976, p. 1877; There was no opportunity to examine this vessel firsthand. The foot is restored in metal, and colleagues have pointed out that one handle is restored. The photograph reproduced here is through the courtesy of *Weltkunst* magazine. It was recently learned that the skyphos was acquired by a private collector.

45. For a discussion of historicizing glass, see A. von Saldern; "Originals-Reproductions-Fakes," *Annales du 5ᵉ Congrès de l'Association Internationale pour l'Histoire du Verre* (Prague 6-11 Juillet 1970), Liège, 1972, pp. 306-313, especially p. 310 on cameo glass; S. M. Goldstein, "Forgeries and Reproductions of Ancient Glass in Corning," *JGS* 19, 1977, pp. 45-49; Revi, *Nineteenth Century Glass*, pp. 170-172; Revi, "Venetian Cameo Glass," *Spinning Wheel* 22, 1966, pp. 10-11 and cover.

46. Eisen, p. 156; Susan Matheson, *Ancient Glass in the Yale University Art Gallery*, New Haven: Yale University, 1980, p. 141, no. A7, mentions the similarity between the figure carved on the Moore Vase (No.87) and Alexandrian relief carving on the Borghese Vase in the Louvre.

47. *Masterpieces*, p. 47, no. 55; *Smith Cat.*, p. 51, no. 56; there are many examples of related plaques in museum and private collections; see p. 16 and footnote 56.

48. For the Moore Vase, footnote 46; for the Curtis Vase, The Toledo Museum of Art, *Deceptions in Glass*, An Exhibition and Pamphlet, no. 4; Eisen, p. 158, calls it the Libbey-Toledo Vase; Eisen, "Antiques," p. 107.

49. Kouchakji in his unpublished manuscript (see footnote 19) acknowledged but refuted Babelon's modern attribution of this vase, E. Babelon, *Catalogue des Camées—Antique et Modernes de la Bibliothèque Nationale*, Paris, 1897, no. 623, pl. 58, fig. 653. At press time, a large transparency and an extensive report on this object were received from Jean-Pierre Catry in Paris. Although we have not seen this object, the material reopens the question of the antiquity of parts of the alabastron.

Fig. 7 *The Naples Vase*,
Roman, early 1st century
A.D., Museo Nazionale,
Naples. Photo Soprinten-
denza Archeologia delle
Province di Napoli e
Caserta.

Museum Bellerive, Zurich,[50] The Museo Vetrario, Venice,[51] and those in the private collections of Pauly & Cie, Venice,[52] and the Rakows (No. 88).

Finally, numerous objects which are now lost or were not really made by the cameo technique as we define it here have not been listed.[53] Specifically, these include the cameo tile of Scaurus which seems to have disappeared.[54] It could be that this plaque along with the Castellani Medusa head[55] may belong to the group of cased and mold-pressed plaques so popular in first century architectural decoration (see p. 15). Although these plaques are usually composed of two contrasting colors, they are not cameo-carved but simply pressed into a mold.[56] Other glasses

Fig. 8 *The Torrita Vase*, Roman, early 1st century A.D., Museo Archeologico, Florence. Photo Soprintendenza alle Antichita d'Eutruria.

such as the Lycurgus cup[57] or the beaker with grapevine garland in the Louvre[58] were not fashioned from cased glass.

I n 1957, eleven museums were listed where collections of cameo fragments were preserved.[59] The list is now outdated, but it is interesting that no major collections of cameo fragments exist in Italian museums. At the time, it was noted that The British Museum in London and The Toledo Museum of Art had the two largest fragment collections. To these two should be added the collection now in The Corning Museum of Glass which consists of some thirty-four fragments acquired from the private collections of Ray Winfield Smith and

50. E. Billeter, *Glas aus der Sammlung des Kunstgewerbemuseums, Zurich*, Sammlungskatalog 4, Zurich: Bruno Kümin, 1969, p. 74, Compagnia di Venezia e Murano, 1887, Inv. no. 3512.

51. A. Dorigato and R. B. Mentasti, *Venezianisches Glas 19. bis 20. Jahrhundert aus dem Glasmuseum Murano, Venedig*, (August bis Oktober 1981-Kunstgewerbemuseum Schloss Köpenick) Berlin, DDR, 1981, p. 14, pl. 4, p. 21, no. 80, a cameo cup attributed to Compagnia di Venezia e Murano, Attilio Spaccarelli, around 1890, also no. 81, the unfinished "Constantine" cup of cameo glass published below; R. B. Mentasti, *Vetri di Murano dell'800*, Venice, 1978, pp. 29, 239, 240; R. Barovier, "Roman Glassware in the Museum of Murano and the Muranese Revival of the Nineteenth Century," *JGS* 16, 1974, p. 116, fig. 9.

52. See Revi references in footnote 45.

53. See p. 13, footnote 38.

54. Eisen, p. 158; Kisa, fig. 193.

55. Eisen, p. 157.

56. See footnote 47; these plaques consist of a greenish translucent backing which has been cased, or more accurately, layered or sandwiched with a strip of translucent deep blue, opaque medium blue, or opaque white glass. This multi-colored strip is pressed into an open mold with the colored layer face down. The resulting plaques and inlays seem to have been popular architectural elements although some are small enough to have been used on furniture.

57. Eisen, pp. 158ff; this vessel, although carved in relief, belongs to the group of late Roman glasses known as *diatreta* or cage-cups. See D. B. Harden and J. M. C. Toynbee, "The Rothschild Lycurgus Cup" *Archaeologia* 97, 1959, pp. 179-212; D. B. Harden, "The Rothschild Lycurgus Cup: Addenda and Corrigenda," *JGS* 5, 1963, pp. 8-17; *Masterpieces*, pp. 77-79, no. 100.

58. Eisen, p. 167; this vessel would seem to have been decorated with some form of "snakethread" technique.

59. Simon, *Portlandvase*, pp. 78-79.

Fig. 9 *Trulla*, Roman, early 1st century A.D., Museo Nazionale, Naples.

Figs. 10, 11 A pair of plaques with Papposilenus and Dionysiac ritual, Roman, early 1st century A.D., Museo Nazionale, Naples. Photo Soprintendenza Archeologia delle Province di Napoli e Caserta.

Giorgio Sangiorgi. A selection of some of the more remarkable examples is represented in the exhibition (Nos. 7-10, 14, 15).

Interestingly, the number of cameo vessel fragments is comparable to the number of complete or nearly complete cameo vessels. When we consider the dozens of costly Roman ribbon glass and mosaic glass vessels preserved in public and private collections worldwide, the small number of cameo vessels stands in marked contrast. Correspondingly, there are *thousands* of mosaic glass and ribbon glass fragments in collections, yet there are probably no more than *two hundred* cameo fragments. A note of caution: more than once, it has been mentioned that *hundreds* of cameo fragments are preserved in one museum or another. The cameo fragments are usually stored with mold-pressed plaques and plaque fragments which are similar in design and color but differ greatly in technique. At a glance all appear to be cameo fragments (this must be the explanation for the inflated numbers). Thus, after eliminating *hundreds* of fragments, it would appear that cameo glasses in the early Roman Empire were nearly as rare as the celebrated *diatreta* of the later Roman Empire.[60]

It is regrettable that only two vessels of this rare and costly cameo technique remain unbroken—The Morgan Cup and the Kofler Bottle. Although other explanations have been offered to account for the rarity of cameo glass objects,[61] these two objects appear to have survived by chance as did other examples of rare glass technique such as gold-glass, painted or enameled glass, and even *diatreta*.

The latest stylistic link in the continuing tradition of cameo glass is the Hunting Bowl (No. 18) found in Switzerland only twelve years ago. It falls between the Roman cameo tradition of the 1st century and the Islamic tradition of the 9th and 10th centuries. The style of the 4th-century bowl is different from the delicate high relief of the early Imperial cameos, yet it hints at the linear relief cutting of the Islamic cameo tradition in both the silhouetting of figures and the colored casing over colorless base.

An economic decline and a change in taste may have caused the demise of cameo glass in first-century Rome, as it actually did in 20th-century England. Future archeological excavation may help expand our current knowledge of later Roman cameo glass production, but for the moment, we must be content with a few fragments and the recently discovered Hunting Bowl.

S.M.G.

---

60. The literature on *diatreta* is continuously growing; see Harden, "Ancient Glass II: Roman," pp. 57-58 and past issues of *JGS*.
61. See page 46.

2. Tiberius
Rome, second quarter of the 1st century A.D.

3. *The Morgan Cup*
Roman, said to have been found at Herakleia in Pontus, second half of the 1st century B.C.

1. **Augustus and Roma**
Rome, first quarter of the 1st century A.D.

5. Portland Vase Disc
Rome (?), first half of the 1st century A.D.

7. Cup or Skyphos (fragment)
Roman, first quarter of the 1st century A.D.

4. Bottle
Roman, said to have been found near Eskis-chehir, Turkey; first quarter of the 1st century A.D., last quarter of the 1st century B.C. Detail above shows figures encircling bottle.

6. The Auldjo Jug
Roman, from Pompeii, late second or third quarter of the 1st century A.D.

8. Six-layered cup
(fragment)
Roman, first half of
the 1st century A.D.

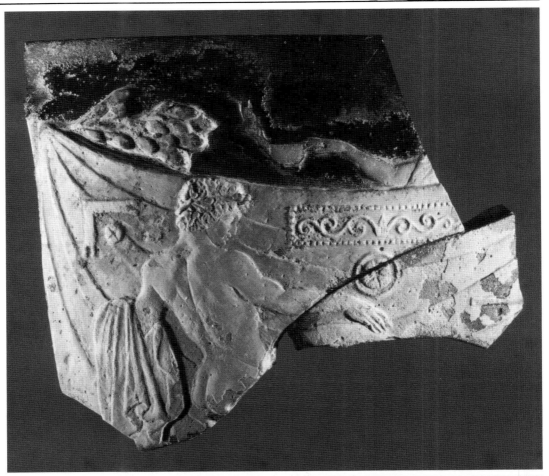

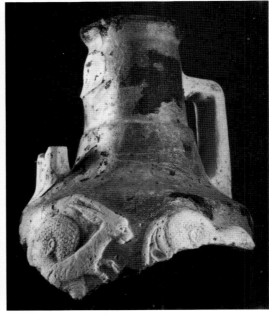

10. Plaque (fragment)
Rome (?) Claudian (?), mid-1st century A.D.

9. Amphoriskos (fragment)
Roman, possibly Alexandria, late 1st century
B.C.-early 1st century A.D.

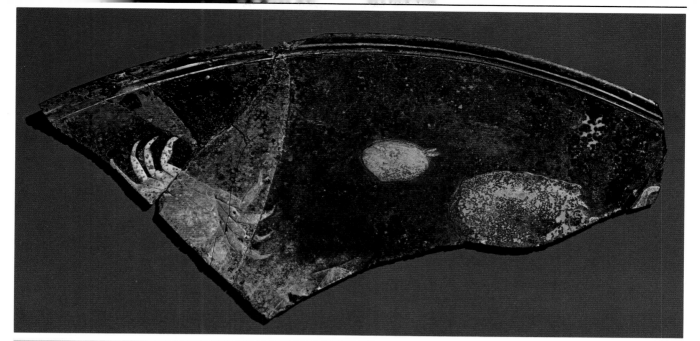

12. Oval Platter (fragment) Roman. said to have been found near the villa of Tiberius on Capri, first half of the 1st century A.D.

11. Cup or Skyphos (fragment)
Roman, first half of the 1st century A.D.

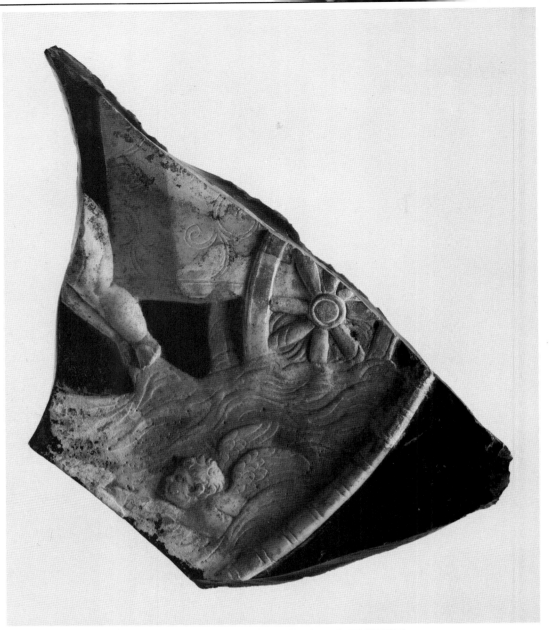

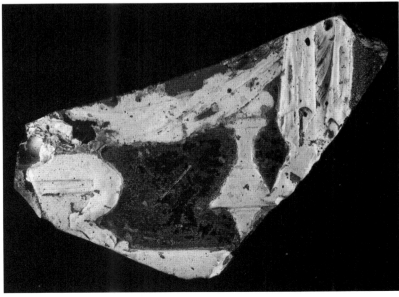

Opposite
14. Large Plaque
(fragment)
Roman, first half of
the 1st century A.D.

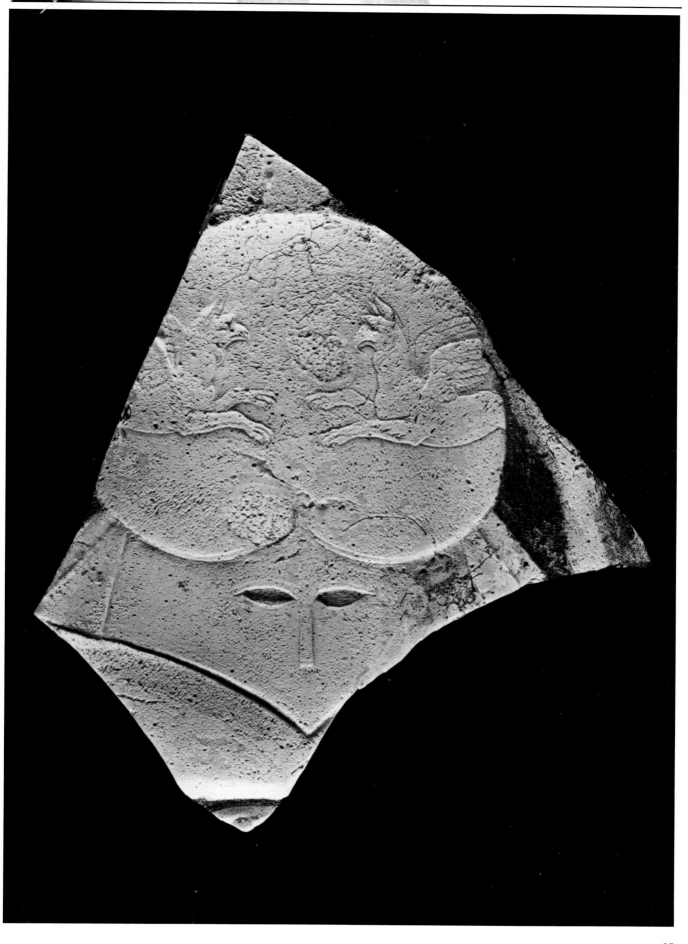

16. Skyphos
Roman, said to have been found in a Parthian
Tomb, Iran, last quarter of the 1st century
B.C.-first quarter of the 1st century A.D.

17. Pitcher or Trefoil Jug
Roman, from Besançon, third quarter of the
1st century A.D.

Opposite
18. Hunting Bowl
Late Roman, from a cemetery at Stein am
Rhein-Burg, second half of the 4th century
A.D.

Islamic Cameo Glass

T oo often the decline of glassmaking in the Roman Empire is seen as an abrupt break in a long tradition, but glassmaking continued at a reduced level in Western Europe and in the "Eastern Byzantine" provinces. The traditions which passed from Rome to Byzantine or Sasanian glassmakers and then to Islamic craftsmen probably occurred smoothly. New trends developed, and new fashions flourished. Techniques such as mosaic glass, once thought to have been lost when Roman glasshouses stopped working, were still in use.[1] Cameo glass, like mosaic glass, continued to be made.

The Islamic tradition of cameo cutting seems to have developed as the engraver acquired technical skills. Unlike Roman vessels, most Islamic cameo vessels appear to have been cut first with a stone wheel to rough out the design, then finished with a rotary, abrasive-fed tool. Thus, while we have consistently referred to Roman objects as being cameo-carved in this catalog, Islamic glass is more accurately described as being "cameo-cut." The latter seems to describe the Late Roman Hunting Bowl (No. 18) in Schaffhausen as well.[2]

Much Islamic glass previously identified as "cameo" is actually made by a marquetry technique. The technique was used to decorate many forms, such as the cylindrical cups already mentioned,[3] flared beakers of the Nishapur-type,[4] small cosmetic dishes,[5] typical globular long-necked bottles,[6] and bottles which imitated metallic forms.[7] The cylindrical cups of the 9th and 10th centuries, such as the Chrysler Museum example (No. 20) in the exhibition, seem first to have had a number of wide stripes of translucent colors applied to the outer surface. Once the vessel was annealed, these areas were cut. The waisted beaker blank (No. 148) in Corning is proof that the forms were covered with wide bands of contrasting colors which were later cut.

Not all Islamic cameo-cut glass was fashioned by this marquetry technique. Outstanding examples of Islamic cameo technique exist and have long been associated with the relief-cutting tradition in Egypt and the Near East. Stylistically, the earliest example of this group is the bell-shaped bottle from the C. L. David Collection in Copenhagen (Fig. 12).[8] The form of the vessel and the characteristically beveled and carefully contoured modeling of the birds suggest a late 9th or early 10th-century date.[9] Compare this shaded, sculptural treatment of the animals with the linear outline-cutting of the gazelles and eagles on the colorless and green ewer (Fig. 13)[10] There, the animals are stylized and attenuated, but the elegance of the carving is unparalleled. The form of the ewer resembles an Egyptian

1. C. J. Lamm, *Das Glas van Samarra*, Berlin, 1928, p. 109, pl. 8, 9; Staatliche Museen Preussischer Kulturbesitz, *Museum für Islamische Kunst Berlin*, Berlin-Dahlem, 1971, p. 54, pl. 5, no. 167; C. Clairmont, "Some Islamic Glass in The Metropolitan Museum" in *Islamic Art in The Metropolitan Museum of Art*, New York, 1972, p. 144, no. 5; *JGS* 19, 1977, p. 170, no. 11, a small bowl (D. 5.4 cm.) in the Corning Museum; there are related unpublished examples in The Toledo Museum of Art and the L. A. Mayer Memorial Institute for Islamic Art, Jerusalem, and the Islamic Dept., British Museum.

2. At the time of printing, there had not been an opportunity to examine the piece, but detailed photography offers no evidence that the surface was worked or polished with hand tools.

3. Kunstmuseum Luzern, p. 140, no. 623; *Smith Cat.*, p. 285, no. 609; Houston, Museum of Fine Arts, *The Art of Glass*, Houston, 1970, p. 8, no. 6; M. Mahboubian, *Treasures of Persian Art after Islam*, New York: Plantin Press, Inc., 1970 (n.p.) no. 1103; Lamm, *Samarra*, p. 68, no. 187, pl. 5.

4. A. v. Saldern, *Glass 500 B.C. to A.D. 1900, The Hans Cohn Collection*, Mainz, 1980, p. 156, no. 149.

5. Kunstmuseum Luzern, p. 120, no. 485, attributed to Amlash, 6-7th century A.D., but this seems unlikely.

6. *Masterpieces*, p. 110, no. 148.

Fig. 12 Bottle with heraldic birds, Islamic cameo glass, late 9th century A.D., C.L. David Collection, Copenhagen.

Fig. 13 Ewer with gazelles and eagles, Islamic cameo glass, 10th century A.D., private collection, England.

Fig. 14 Bowl with gazelles, Islamic cameo glass, 10th century A.D., Museum of Islamic Art, Cairo.

Fatamid rock crystal piece, but a Persian origin has been suggested for the place of manufacture.[11] Compared with the few examples of cameo-cut glasses from Egypt, this ewer is certainly more refined and carefully executed. The boldly-cut, stylized ibexes on the bowl in the Islamic Museum, Cairo (Fig. 14), relate to the eagle and gazelle on the ewer.[12] A mid-10th century date seems reasonable for both vessels as well as for the cylindrical cup in Jerusalem (No. 19) and the handled jug (No. 21). Note that a drill was used to stipple or dot the body of the animals on the cup and the jug. This internal dot pattern is a very late feature; objects with such decoration may even date to the 11th century.[13] Considerable numbers of relief-cut glasses have been excavated recently; new studies of relief-cut styles will certainly add to our knowledge of the extraordinary quality of Islamic cameo-cut glass.

S.M.G.

7. Davids Samling, pp. 19-20; A. von Saldern *JGS* 15, 1973, p. 191, no. 17; *Meisterwerke Der Glaskunst Aus internationalem Privatbesitz*, Düsseldorf, 1968, p. 22, no. 39; A. v. Saldern, "Sassanadische und Islamische Gläser in Düsseldorf und Hamburg," *Jahrbuch der Hamburger Kunstsammlungen*, 13, 1968, p. 52, fig. 11.

8. *Arts of Islam*, p. 140, no. 131; Davids Samling, pp. 17-18; *JGS* 14, 1972, p. 155, no. 21; C. L. Davids Samling, *Fjerde del Jubilaeumsskrift 1945-70* (ed. A. Leth), Copenhagen, 1970, pp. 138-139, no. 18.

9. Oliver, *JGS* 3, pp. 9-29 for a discussion of chronology.

10. Translucent green over colorless glass, broken and repaired, H. 15.5 cm, decorated with eagles attacking gazelles, repeated in heraldic position; behind each a long parrot fills the space near the elaborately cut handle, private collection, England; *Arts of Islam*, p. 141, no. 132, color plate, p. 54.

11. Robert Charleston is currently working on the publication of this ewer.

12. Translucent deep blue over colorless glass with a greenish tinge, two large fragments, H. 8.5 cm; D. 12 cm; cameo cut and drilled to decorate bodies of ibexes, Kufic inscription reads "Felicity, glory (? to God?) to its owner"; *Arts of Islam*, p. 140, no. 130; Ministry of Culture, UAR, *Islamic Art in Egypt 969-1517*, Cairo, 1969, p. 170, no. 159; Lamm, *Mitt. Gläser*, p. 165, pl. 61.10 and for earlier bibliography.

13. Oliver, *op. cit.*, pp. 24-25.

20. Cup with stylized tree
Islamic, Iran (?), late 9th-10th century

21. Jug or Pitcher (fragments)
Islamic, said to be from Iran, late 10th century

19. Cup with Gazelles
Islamic, said to have been found at Nishapur,
Iran, mid-10th century

Chinese Cameo Glass

T The Hunting Bowl (No. 18) provides a tenuous but interesting link between the cameo glass of the 1st century and that of the 9th and 10th centuries. Is there a comparable link between Islamic and Chinese cameo? We know that the Chinese had contact with both the Roman and Islamic world. Roman glass was treasured in China in the 3rd and 4th centuries, but there are no known references to early cameo glass having been found in China. Islamic glass makers were unquestionably influenced by Chinese art in the 13th and 14th centuries, and enameled glasses reflect a Chinese influence as goods were imported from and exported to China while it was ruled by the Mongols. Several of the re markable Islamic enameled glasses at the Freer Gallery of Art in Washington, D.C., were acquired in China.[1] Is the popularity of the marquetry technique in both Islam and China somehow related?

The second Qing (Ch'ing) ruler, Kangzi (K'ang-hsi) (1662–1722) set up workshops for the production of glass in the palace complex at Beijing (Peking). However, there is no evidence that the palace workshops produced *any* cameo glass at this early date.

The palace workshops were directed by European missionaries, and some writers have suggested that the material produced at this early date was atypical for Chinese glass and had not yet developed into a mature or characteristic style.[2] The founding of the glass factory at Boshan (Poshan) in Shandong (Shantung) province is somewhat later, and there is general agreement that much of the characteristic cameo glass, including snuff bottles, may have been produced there in the 18th century.[3] By the 19th century, Boshan had been making glass for a century. With this long history, the emergence of cameo carving and marquetry decoration seems to have occurred in the early 18th century.[4] Considering that no marks are known on cameo-carved vessels before the Qianlong (Ch'ien-lung) Emperor (1736–1795), the initiation of the technique might reasonably be assigned to this period.[5] In dis cussing the history of snuff bottles, Hugh Moss has pointed out that ruby-red glass was introduced shortly before 1705 and that it, along with yellow, was associated with the Imperial Court.[6]

Glass bottles of all and every shape and color are made to contain it (snuff). The colors are red, purple, yellow, white, black, and green; the white is like crystal and the red like fire. Things of great delight . . . they are all manufactured within the palace. Imitations are made by the common people but they never attain the standard of the original. (from Wang Shizhen, *Xiangzu biji*, 1705).

The account of crystal and fire is a dramatic yet appropriate description of the Warrior Vase (No. 34). The rocky landscape undulates like flames, and the shrub bery appears to billow like rising smoke. The cutting style, even more than the color combination, seems to illustrate the words of the early 18th-century writer. It would seem that this color combination of translucent red over colorless glass which has the appearance of crushed ice or simple opaque white was most charac teristic of Chinese cameo glass in the 18th century. The Warrior Vase, in size and technical virtuosity, is the acknowledged masterpiece of its type.

1. E. Atil, *Renaissance of Islam: Art of the Mamluks*, Washington, D.C., 1981, p. 120.
2. Plesch, "Chinese Glass," pp. 73–76; he refers to those early forms as "pool glasses" while more typical forms are "main stream."
3. Bushell, p. 62ff; H. Moss, *Snuff Bottles of China*, London, 1971, p. 36; Plesch, "Chinese Glass," p. 76.
4. Bushell, p. 67.

It has been suggested that Boshan produced not only finished products but raw materials and uncarved cameo blanks for distribution to other centers where lapidaries were working.[7] One need only compare the wide range of carving quality in the cameo technique to realize that many craftsmen were producing objects at many aesthetic levels. Was the quality of carving a result of some lapidaries' inability to do better work or simply the need to produce large quantities of second quality material? If we are to accept the writings of Wang Shizhen in the early 18th century, then the latter need and the production of glass for both the Imperial family and the common man must be the answer.

It is difficult to accept the recent proposal that most cameo glass was made for export to the West.[8] This theory is based on the lack of any documentation which acknowledges that the Chinese themselves accepted or used cameo glass. The point may be argued from both sides, but the "non-European" color combinations and the characteristically Chinese shape or function of many cameo glasses would suggest that a local use was intended. That many pieces *were* exported is certain; that they were *made* for export seems less clear. Certainly, the English produced cameo glass in the oriental style (Nos. 81-86) so effectively that it was sometimes attributed to China.

The cameo glass in this catalog was included to illustrate a wide range of color, shape, and carving technique. The selection of snuff bottles from the Marian Swayze Mayer Collection offers, in miniature, the breadth and range of the lapidary's art as expressed in glass in China. It has been pointed out that it is difficult to date glass snuff bottles exactly. This is also true of Chinese glass in general. Perhaps this exhibition will renew an interest among students to re-examine this problem.

S.M.G.

5. Plesch, "Chinese Glass," p. 77.

6. Moss, *ibid.*, p. 36; Moss, *Snuff Bottle Exhibition.*

7. Moss, *Snuff Bottle Exhibition,*

8. Warren, "Chinese Glass," p. 117.

23-27. Snuff Bottles,
Chinese, 1780-1920

28. Hookah Base or vase
Chinese, 1768-1769

22. Ginger Jar
Chinese, 1736-1795, Qianlong mark

30-31. Vase in the form of a fish and Rouge box
Chinese, 18th century, probably Qianlong
(1736-1795)

34. The Warrior Vase
China, 18th century, probably Qianlong
(1735-1796)

29. Bottle
Chinese, 18th century, probably Qianlong
(1735-1796)

32. Bottle
Chinese, 18th century, probably Qianlong
(1735-1796)

33. Pot
Chinese, 18th century, probably Qianlong
(1735-1796)

Like Venus rising from the waves at Cythera full grown, so did English cameo glass burst upon the Victorian scene in 1876. Yet, in a mere fifty years the style had peaked, exhausted its exotic, glamorous life span, and disappeared as had its ancient cameo glass progenitor 2000 years before. That reawakened interest in cameo glass which inspired the revival, caused it to flame so furiously and disappear so quickly, continues to excite all who love the great creations of glass.

It was Benjamin Richardson, known as "The Father of the Glass Trade," who blazed the way to the rebirth of cameo glass. With the repeal of the stifling Excise Duty in 1845, the glass industry of England began to emerge from its economic restrictions. The removal of the tax sparked change and innovation and allowed for experimentation and progress. At Stourbridge, where the English glass industry had centered since the 17th century, Thomas Webb and Benjamin Richardson and William Haden Richardson entered into the partnership of Webb & Richardson in 1829 to form the Wordsley Glass Works. In 1836, Thomas left the partnership to found the firm that would become Thomas Webb & Sons. The third Richardson brother, Jonathan, then joined the firm, which became known as W. H., B. & J. Richardson. By 1852 this firm discontinued its existence, and in 1853 it carried only the name of Benjamin Richardson. By 1863 it was known as Hodgetts, Richardson & Son. Benjamin Richardson died in 1887 at the age of 85.

For forty years Benjamin Richardson had been the beacon light that helped to guide the destinies of many great glass craftsmen. His leadership and his inventiveness resulted in the recreation of cameo glass. His willingness to tread new pathways and his stimulating personality inspired the many young craftsmen who worked for him and with him in those creative years.

Among the many fine young decorators, designers, etchers, and carvers who matured under the influence of Richardson were John Northwood I, Philip Pargeter, Joseph Locke, Alphonse Lechevrel, William J. Muckley, and Thomas Bott (uncle of the Woodall brothers). It was Richardson who brought a Wedgwood copy of the Portland Vase to inspire his young craftsmen. It was he who offered £1000 to anyone who could produce it in glass. It was this stimulus that led Pargeter and Northwood to create a glass replica of the most famous of all ancient cameo glass pieces, the Portland Vase.

Thomas Carlyle, in his book *Heroes and Hero Worship*, discusses whether the leader creates the times or the times create the leader. If Richardson were the leader who helped to create the times, then certainly it was the times that made John Northwood I the leader. Northwood was born in Wordsley, Staffordshire, in 1836. At the age of twelve he was already working for the firm of W. H., B. & J. Richardson of Wordsley, decorating, gilding, and enameling glass. After that factory closed in 1852, he was hired by Benjamin Richardson the very next year when his factory reopened. When the Stourbridge Government School of Design opened in September of 1852, John Northwood attended, like the other keen apprentices of his time, even though it meant giving up his evenings after long hours on the job. Northwood was awarded a medal by the School of Design in 1855.

He left Benjamin Richardson's employ in 1859 and formed a partnership with his brother Joseph, H. G. Richardson, and T. Guest. The partnership was dissolved a year later and replaced with only Northwood's brother as partner in a firm then known as J. & J. Northwood. Joseph was the businessman and administrator; John concentrated on the technical and developmental aspects. From the beginning, the business was successful and grew rapidly as John Northwood's inventiveness and leadership emerged. Many men later prominent in glass history worked for J. & J. Northwood and trained in the Northwood techniques, among them George and Thomas Woodall, James Hill, and Edwin Grice. A cutting shop was added and a special steam boiler constructed not only to heat the building but also to make special provision for melting pans which held the paints, varnishes, and the beeswax needed to coat the glass for etching. In 1861 Northwood invented the Template Etching machine which produced mechanical decoration by tracing through the openings in the templates into the wax coating on the glass. Grice made the wooden patterns for this machine. Immersion of the glass in acid then produced the etching. This labor-saving device was soon followed by the invention of the Geometrical Etching machine which did not require templates. Several other innovations were developed by Northwood. Purely by experimental trial and error, John Northwood developed "white acid" which dissolved only the glass surface and did not eat into the glass as did the pure hydrofluoric acid. Thus he could complete the details within his etched designs and no longer required the services of an engraver.

The deep engraving techniques developed by Bohemian craftsmen such as August Böhm had already begun to influence English glass makers, and Northwood was no exception. In 1864, J. B. Stone commissioned Northwood to carve the Elgin Vase (Fig. 15) now in The Birmingham Art Gallery. The tools and techniques used for this endeavor were entirely of his own invention. The tools first designed and used for carving cameo glass by John Northwood consisted essentially of small tempered steel rods from 1/16 to 1/8 inch in diameter, driven into a soft wooden pencil-sized holder (No. 155). The steel and wood were ground together to a long triangular point on a stone, the three edges being very sharp. These were later improved so that the steel lay in a hollow metal handle with jaws (No. 156) and was fed to the jaws as it was worn away and resharpened. The thumb of the left hand steadied the piece against a bran pad while the thumb and the first two fingers of the right held the tool which cut the glass. Great strength and dexterity were required. Small files and riffles were used to smooth the carving and to enhance details. When the Elgin Vase was completed in 1873, it was hailed by English critics as the most important glass object made since the Roman era. The frieze around the body of the vase, representing two equestrian groups from the Parthenon sculptures, was carved in bas-relief and polished. It was the forerunner of what would become the English "Rock Crystal" style, an engraved, deeply cut and polished glass with the same clarity and brilliance of natural rock crystal. The result of Northwood's success and that of others such as Frederick E. Kny and William Fritsche established this decorating technique.

The first cameo piece done by John Northwood I, begun four years before the Elgin vase was started, was a small trial cameo glass vase; the opal or opaque white glass was carved in relief on a colored glass body with Perseus and Andromeda in the style of a St. George and the Dragon; a pencil tracing of this design by John Northwood I was among Kenneth Northwood's papers (Fig. 16). Undoubtedly this was the first piece of 19th-century glass cameo, executed about 1860. Unfortunately, it was accidentally broken some years later.

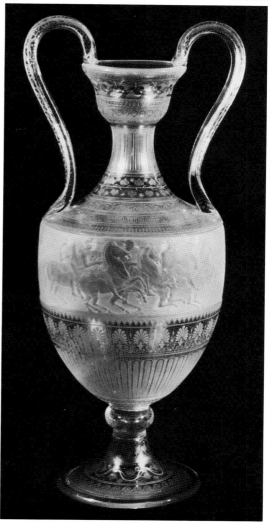

Fig. 15 *The Elgin Vase*, England, 1873, John Northwood I, "Rock Crystal style," Birmingham Museum of Art. Photo Birmingham Museum of Art, Birmingham.

The stage was now set: the man and the times had come together. One more ingredient was added—Philip Pargeter, Northwood's cousin, owner of the Red House Glass Works at Wordsley. Pargeter, nephew of Richardson, had also been employed and influenced by Richardson. He, too, saw the Portland Vase as a superlative achievement. He now took up the Richardson challenge and offered £1000 to Northwood if he would carve a replica of the Portland on a blank that he, Pargeter, would produce. Northwood agreed, and Pargeter had a precise blank made at his Red House Glass Works by Daniel Hancock. The cameo glass cycle would begin again by duplicating the most complex and famous piece of the ancient world, the Portland Vase. There were many trips to the British Museum to compare Northwood's vase with the original, and one of his many sketches of the Portland Vase is illustrated in Kenneth Northwood's papers (Fig. 17). The task was not easy, and it would be three long years before Northwood's copy of the Portland Vase was completed in 1876. Northwood labored on his great work every moment he could spare from his very busy decorating and etching business.

In addition to all his other activities, Northwood spent as much time as possible in museums in both England and France. He was fascinated by classical objects and filled countless books with designs based on ancient engraved objects.

In 1876, three years after he began, Northwood completed his Portland Vase (No. 35). Although the vase had cracked on one of its last journeys to London for comparison with the original, public enthusiasm for it was not dampened. Northwood repaired the broken vase and completed the carving and polishing. The Northwood Portland was the first important piece of cameo glass to be made in the 19th century, and it matched the best of the ancient world. It elicited immediate praise and world-wide acclaim. Northwood, Pargeter, and Stourbridge were famous. At once there was great demand for cameo-carved glass objects.

Pargeter immediately commissioned the Milton Vase (No. 36), which depicted the Archangel Michael in the Garden of Eden on one side and Adam and Eve on the other. This vase was followed by four tazzas representing Art, Literature, Science, and Engineering. The Flaxman tazza (No. 37) represented Art, the Shakespeare tazza (No. 38) Literature, the Newton tazza (No. 39) Science, but the fourth, of James Watt to represent Engineering, was never completed. Only the pencil drawing (Fig. 18) done by Northwood remains.

In the past few years, a second Shakespeare tazza (No. 40) by Northwood, previously unknown, has appeared. The

Fig. 16 Perseus and Andromeda, pencil on tracing paper, John Northwood I, about 1860; study for his first cameo glass vessel. Collection of Dr. and Mrs. Leonard S. Rakow.

other tazzas have a short threaded bolt imbedded in the center of the back so that they can be attached either to a cameo glass foot (Fig. 20) or to a blue, velvet-colored frame (Fig. 19). The frames were cleverly designed by Northwood: the backing is mirrored so that light passing through the translucent blue glass of each tazza is reflected back to highlight the blue glass around each carved head. The recently discovered Shakespeare tazza has only a jagged stump of broken glass at the center of the back. Over it, a modern foot has been cemented (Fig. 21). The blue color has been so well matched that it is hard to realize it is not the intended original; the white border of the added foot has apparently been trailed on and has not been carved. Recorded on a photograph of the Flaxman tazza, written in pencil on the back, is the following: "There was to be a fourth tazza but it was not

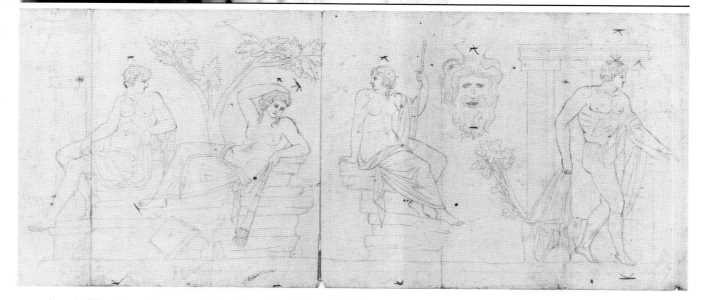

Fig. 17 *The Portland Vase*, pencil on paper, John Northwood I, about 1870; preliminary sketches. Collection of Dr. and Mrs. Leonard S. Rakow.

completed. The foot [damaged] [and repaired] is unfinished and in John Northwood II's studio." Is this a reference to the newly discovered second Shakespeare tazza? It *may* refer to an unknown, unfinished tazza of James Watt, the Scottish inventor.

The Flaxman tazza is signed ⋈ "1880." The Newton tazza is signed "J. Northwood 1878" in script, but neither the original Shakespeare nor the newly discovered one is signed at all. It is interesting that on the Flaxman tazza Northwood used the same ⋈ monogram he used to sign the fifteen jasperware Portland vases he polished for Wedgwood *after* he had completed his cameo glass Portland.

The cameo-carved tazza borders are all different (Fig. 22). The Flaxman tazza has a border of holly leaves, flowers, and berries; the Newton tazza has a border of ivy leaves and berries, and the Shakespeare tazza has a border of oak leaves and acorns. The recently discovered Shakespeare tazza has a border of laurel leaves and small buds.

Northwood's last known cameo object is the Pegasus or Dennis Vase, (No. 41), finished in 1890 and now in the Smithsonian Institution, Gellatly Collection. It was created because Mr. Wilkes Webb of Thomas Webb & Sons, Dennis Glass Works, wanted a vase that would help to identify his firm as a leader in the field. It would be the largest of the cameo glass objects carved by Northwood. In three parts—foot, body, and cover—the vase had a domed lid with an opal glass Pegasus finial; the horse-head handles of the body were carved of the same glass. Aurora was depicted on one side of the vase, Amphitrite on the other; there are ten figures shown in all. Despite its unfinished state, it was awarded a Gold Medal at the Paris Exhibition of 1878.

Edwin Grice (1839-1913), who worked with J. & J. Northwood for eighteen years before leaving to join Guest Brothers, assisted with the Portland Vase and may have carved the handles; he is known to have made the special carrying case for the Portland Vase. He roughed out the horse-head handles and the Pegasus finial atop the Pegasus Vase.

A small glass Shakespeare pendant carved by John Northwood I should be mentioned. It is of a white opal on a dark background and is worn by Mrs. Kenneth Northwood, wife of John Northwood's grandson, as a pendant on a bracelet (Fig. 23). These eight objects, then, are the total of John Northwood I's cameo glass creations. All of his major cameo pieces have been brought together in this exhibition for the first time.

Fig. 18 James Watt, pencil on paper, John Northwood I, about 1880; study for a tazza representing engineering. Collection of Dr. and Mrs. Leonard S. Rakow.

The art of the *diatretarius*, who carved the cameo, had been practiced intermittently for 2000 years in the western world. What had happened to the carving of cameo glass? Hundreds of shards lie in museums around the world, but only two complete pieces are preserved from the Roman era. We feel the problem lies in the physical properties of cased glass although not everyone agrees (see p. 9). Unequal coefficients of expansion and contraction will cause cracking or separation as temperature changes make the glass expand or contract even if these coefficients of expansion and contraction are almost equal. A darker glass will lose or gain heat at a rate different from that of a lighter glass. Tension and stresses occur daily with normal changes in temperature. It is small wonder there is little intact ancient cameo glass today. The ancients had neither pyrometers (to measure furnace temperature) nor sophisticated chemistry to assist them.

It appears that once a glassmaker decided to case glass, he repeated the mistakes of his predecessors, for the literature is replete with losses incurred when glass was cased. Every glassblower can relate his many difficulties in casing glass. Some glassmakers leave their cased glass untouched for months to determine if it will survive daily changes in temperature. The reason that so little ancient cameo glass survives intact today may be that daily temperature changes over 2000 years and the shocks incidental to use and handling have left us with only the shards and broken vessels of the ancient glassmakers. It is unfortunate enough to have cased glass self-destruct shortly after it has cooled; it was even worse to endure the anger of the buyers if the glass flew into pieces only weeks or months after purchase.

We must not proclaim that the correct procedure for making cameo glass has been found. Far from it! It may take 1000 years to determine if the cased glass of the 19th century will withstand the vicissitudes of time. This problem also beset the cameo glass industry in Stourbridge. Breakage of cased glass was enormous, but even more catastrophic was the cracking of cased glass after carving had begun. After all, Northwood's great Portland Vase replica cracked before it was completed. Recently, at Dema Glass, successor to Thomas Webb & Sons, it was reported that the cameo glass frames on the portrait medallions of the Winans, in the T. Webb & Sons Museum, spontaneously cracked in many places while stored in a bank vault. They are only *100* years old!

Despite these physical problems, in 1880, when Northwood became Art Director and Works Manager at Brierley Hill, the popularity of cameo glass increased tremendously. At Stevens & Williams, every available engraver was kept working long hours, six days a week. Northwood's ingenuity in producing cased glass with compatible coefficients of expansion allowed the firm to reduce loss in this rapidly expanding industry.

Northwood devised a means to determine coefficients of expansion so that the cased glasses would be compatible. He developed an expansion-testing machine with steam as the source of heat and a dial to measure the expansion mechanically. Time, money, and effort were saved as a result of this invention, but many factors had to be considered. Both the coefficients of expansion and contraction were vital to the stability of cased glass. Careful annealing was of utmost importance; heat had to be dissipated slowly as the glass passed critical points in its cooling. Glass with a greater expansion coefficient can be used more safely as the inner layer when ratios are unequal since less stress will develop in the cooling stage. A thinner inner layer reduces stress considerably.

Stevens & Williams, now Royal Brierley Crystal, had been formed by William Stevens and Samuel Cox Williams in 1847. Both were married to daughters of Joseph Silvers who had previously leased the Brierley Hill Glass Works. In 1870 a new glass factory was constructed, and the guiding force during this creative period was Joseph Silvers Williams-Thomas (1864-1933); he was followed by his son, Hubert.

At Stevens & Williams, a skilled group of glassmakers specialized in making cased glass, and many new shapes and color effects were designed and developed. The great demand for cameo glass required meticulous engraving; in order to reduce this to a minimum, the outer layer of casing was made as thin as possible. Less time and money could be expended, not only in removing the excess glass from the outer layer but also in carving what remained.

Others in the Northwood family contributed greatly to the cameo glass industry. John Northwood II improved the accuracy of his father's expansion-testing machine by testing two rods in a vertical position simultaneously, using controlled gas heat, and by registering changes in expansion on a large dial. His grandson, Kenneth Northwood, improved this apparatus still further by utilizing electrical heat and providing an even more sensitive mirror indicator on a large scale. By substituting the mirror indicator for the old mechanical indicator, the apparatus was made much more sensitive.

William Northwood, 1857-1937, a nephew of John Northwood, was noted for his copper plate engraving, his photography, and his cameo glass carving. One amazing aspect of this remarkably gifted man was that his left arm was completely paralyzed from birth. Sam Thompson, who worked with William Northwood as a youth and is still at Royal Brierley Crystal, remembers that William would lift his paralyzed left arm and place it across the object he was carving to help hold it in place. If extra steadiness was required, he would hold a bran-filled sack against the object with his chin. At the Stevens & Williams Museum there is a beautiful example of his carved floral cameo work and a terra cotta molded piece he made as a pattern for his glass work. A broken plaque of his

Fig. 22 Detail of border designs; (top to bottom), Flaxman, No. 37; Shakespeare, No. 38; Newton, No. 39; Shakespeare, No. 40.

Venus and Dancing Cupid can be seen at the Broadfield House Glass Museum. Another of his plaques, *Venus Instructing Cupid* (No. 42), was sent to Canada for safekeeping during World War II and was accidentally sold for U.S. dollars at its pound-insured price. It disappeared for thirty years and then surfaced in New York where it was acquired for the Rakow collection along with a letter of authenticity from John Northwood II.

Fig. 23 Shakespeare pendant, John Northwood I, after 1880. Collection of Mr. and Mrs. Kenneth Northwood. Photo Dr. Leonard S. Rakow.

John Northwood II, 1870-1960, also played an important role in cameo glass and in the history of the Stourbridge area. If ever there was an individual *born* into the cameo glass tradition, that person was John Northwood II. His heritage, education, and environment totally immersed him in this field. At the age of fifteen, he was already at work in the cameo department of Stevens & Williams. By seventeen, at the urging of his father, he began his master work, *Aphrodite and Attendants* (No. 43). He did not finish it until after the death of his father, sixteen years later. It is a sixteen-inch plaque of opaque white over colorless on ruby glass. After it had received its polishing with Joshua Hodgetts' aid, it fell from the table, broke, but was subsequently repaired.

Northwood II succeeded his father as Art Director and Works Manager at Stevens & Williams in 1902. He studied European and American methods of glassmaking and supervised mass production of many types of colorless and colored glass. In 1958 he wrote a biography of his father, John Northwood I, which detailed much of the glass history of the times. He also contributed a great many of the items now on display at the Broadfield House Glass Museum. Although he was involved with the production of commercial cameo glass, he himself carved very little. His plaque, *Dancing Figures*, was sent to Canada for safekeeping during World War II and disappeared.

Dr. G. C. Campbell, who attended Northwood II in his last illness, was given a Northwood II vase (Fig. 24) by members of the Northwood family. Cameo decoration of a lake with two men rowing a boat, a forest, and mountains encircles the piece. Kenneth Northwood remembers seeing his father working on this vase. On its way to the United States in 1976, the vase was stolen. If it has not been destroyed and does appear again, we hope it will be recognized. Misfortune seems to have dogged the steps of the three documented figural cameo pieces of John Northwood II. Only the *Aphrodite and Attendants* has survived.

Not only the Northwoods made cameo glass history at Stevens & Williams. Joshua Hodgetts (1858-1933), born in Kingswinford, attended the Stourbridge School of Art at night. He was first employed by J. & J. Northwood but later shifted to Stevens & Williams where he worked for forty years. He was well-known for the realism of his floral and bird carvings (No. 94). Typical of his extraordinary work is the cameo glass portrait medallion of Joseph Silvers.

James Benjamin Hill (1850-1928), another cameo glass carver, was employed by J. & J. Northwood at Wordsley at the age of eleven. He later worked for Northwood at Stevens & Williams. Two unfinished twelve-inch plaques were begun by him about 1880: one is white on a ruby background, the other, white on a light blue background (No. 44). The latter plaque shows the heroic figure of a knight fighting the devil. An unfinished small white-on-red vase signed by Hill is illustrated to show the technique of acid cutting (No. 154).

In 1877, Richardson brought Alphonse Eugène Lechevrel, a French medalist and gem engraver, to Wordsley to train workers at the Richardson Glass Factory in the technique of cameo carving. Six major figural cameo glass vases are attributed to Lechevrel of which four are still known to exist. Two of these, the white-on-blue Venus vases (Nos. 45 and 46) have been brought together again after 100 years—

for the first time since they were shown at the Paris Exposition in 1878 and at the Worcester Exhibition in 1882 (Fig. 25). At that time both had handles and both bore Lechevrel's signature. One, from the collection of the Broadfield House Glass Museum, is still signed "AL 1878," but both are now also signed "George Woodall." In addition to having the handles ground off both, the opal at the foot seems to have had some additional carving. Close inspection of the vase from the Rakow collection shows that the Lechevrel signature was removed. A small crack in the opal exactly matches one in the photo of the same vase when it had handles, which further establishes its identity.

Joseph Locke (1846-1936) was apprenticed at age twelve as a designer and decorator in the Royal Worcester China Factory. After winning a design competition, he joined Guest Brothers in Stourbridge only to leave them for Hodgetts and Richardson. There, under the tutelage of Lechevrel, he became an excellent cameo glass carver. For the 1878 Paris Exhibition, he carved a second replica of the Portland Vase (No. 47). Of forty blanks made for him, thirty-eight were either defective or cracked after carving had begun. The thirty-ninth was satisfactory and intact after carving, and when it was shown in a not-quite-complete state at the Paris Exhibition, it was awarded a gold medal. The white opal figures were never completely thinned down; Locke left Richardson, first for Pargeter, then for Webb and Corbett and, finally, for the New England Glass Company in America in 1882. The fortieth Portland blank (No. 152) still travels with the Locke Portland.

In addition to the second Portland replica, Locke is known to have completed two cameo glass vases now at the Chrysler Museum, *The Happy Child* and *The Unhappy Child*, and a small classical head in the Rakow Collection. Several photographs of four other cameo glass vases attributed to Locke do prove that others may exist. One of them, *Cupid Sailing on a Cockleshell* (No. 48), was last seen at the opening of the Wordsley Art School in 1899 and has since been located. The others are still being sought.

It is not known if Locke carved any cameo glass while in the United States, although he was quite successful as a glassmaker and invented many new types of glass. One cameo glass vase signed by him, with floral decoration, is in the Museum of Fine Arts, Boston, but was probably made while he was still in England.

Frederick Engelbert Kny, William Fritsche, H. J. Boam, and Franz Joseph Palme were among the Bohemian glass artists who worked for Thomas Wilkes Webb. Both Fritsche and Kny soon made distinguished contributions to the English Rock Crystal style. Although they carved cameo glass, they did little figural work and rarely signed their glass. One well-documented plaque carved by Frederick Kny's son, Ludwig, is known (No. 52), and one plaque is signed by Boam (No. 51).

Fredrick Carder (1863-1963) followed his father in the pottery industry but was so influenced by Northwood's cameo glass Portland Vase that he became a glassmaker. After a year of instruction at J. & J. Northwood, and on Northwood's recommendation, he joined Stevens & Williams in 1880. When Northwood became Art Director and Manager at Stevens & Williams in 1881, he continued to shape the genius of Carder. There are many examples of Carder's modeling in many different materials. While Northwood was completing his Pegasus Vase, Carder

Fig. 24 Cameo vase, John Northwood II, woodland scenes; stolen 1976. Photo Dr. Leonard S. Rakow.

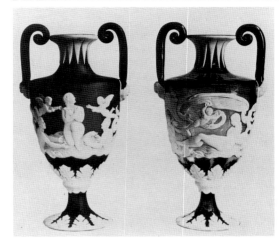

Fig. 25 Photograph, pair of vases, Alphonse Lechevrel, 1878; photographed around the time of the Paris Exhibition.

carved his plate, *Immortality of the Arts* (No. 49). In 1903, Carder left Stevens & Williams and went to the United States to work for Thomas Hawkes and manage Steuben Glass Works, which became a Corning Glass subsidiary in 1918. Carder remained Director at Steuben until 1933, after which he became Art Director at Corning and maintained a private studio from which came new glass creations and many worthwhile experiments.

Thomas Webb founded Thomas Webb & Sons in 1837 after he dissolved his partnership with the Richardsons. He purchased the Dennis estate at Amblecote in 1856 and built a new glass house. After Thomas Webb's death, his three sons, Thomas Wilkes Webb, Charles Webb, and Walter Wilkes Webb headed the firm. Thomas Wilkes Webb was the leader of the group. He commissioned the "Dennis" Vase and saw to it that the company hired and trained the finest glass artists.

Jules Barbe, gilder and enameler, was brought to Webb from Paris by T.W. Webb in 1878 and remained there for twenty-one years. He developed a special technique for decorating cameo glass that required several firings and burnishings; three objects are shown here (Nos. 77, 79, 80). He teamed with F. Kretschman, another fine cameo glass carver, to produce an elaborate gourd vase (No. 78).

Daniel Pearce, born in 1819, and his son Lionel, born in 1852, affiliated with Webb in 1884 after leaving their decorating business in London. They are well-known for their imitations of Chinese snuff bottles (Nos. 82, 83). They executed many fine simulated-ivory carved vases, and Lionel designed one of the polar bear vases carved by George Woodall.

John Thomas Fereday and James M. O'Fallon were skillful cameo carvers who can be identified among a host of anonymous artists. The famous "Woodall team" photograph (Fig. 26), from Alice Woodall's photograph album kept by her father,

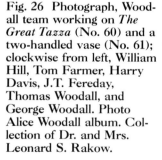

Fig. 26 Photograph, Woodall team working on *The Great Tazza* (No. 60) and a two-handled vase (No. 61); clockwise from left, William Hill, Tom Farmer, Harry Davis, J.T. Fereday, Thomas Woodall, and George Woodall. Photo Alice Woodall album. Collection of Dr. and Mrs. Leonard S. Rakow.

is illustrated. Harry Davis, Tom Farmer, William Hill, and J.T. Fereday are seen with George and Thomas Woodall grouped around *The Great Tazza* (No. 60). Their five-layered cameo glass tazza is a tour de force of cameo glass carving. It has had only three owners since it was originally purchased from T. Webb & Sons by T. Goode & Co and was a prominent feature of the Goode & Co. showrooms for more than half a century. It was pictured there in an 1891 photograph (Fig. 27).

George Woodall (1850-1925) and Thomas Woodall (1849-1926) were born in Kingswinford. The famous Worcester enameler, Thomas Bott, was their uncle; it was he who saw to it that his young nephews attended the Stourbridge School of Art. At the age of twelve, they were employed by

Fig. 27 Photograph, showroom of Thomas Goode & Co., 1871, with *The Great Tazza* (No. 60) and two tricolor lamp bases (No. 76). Collection of Dr. and Mrs. Leonard S. Rakow.

J. & J. Northwood as apprentices and transferred to Thomas Webb & Sons about 1874. In an environment where glass creativity was a way of life, they trained under Northwood, the man who first reproduced cameo glass. The Woodalls' natural talents and constantly improving skills led them to the development of new techniques in Rock Crystal carving. Queen Victoria is said to have purchased their first twenty pieces.

George soon left Thomas behind and developed an unmatched sculptural skill as he devoted his life to the painstaking art form which he brought to its pinnacle. The strength and the vitality of his carving improved constantly. He took no short cuts and carved only the most difficult figural subjects. He had an amazing talent not only for perspective but also for incorporating such fine details that they often could be seen only by magnification.

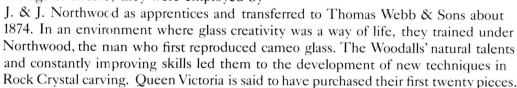

Many other figural pieces (Nos. 61 to 75) illustrate Woodall's tremendous technical skill and artistic excellence. Enlargements made from small areas of his cameo carving reveal this technical mastery. On the *Shepherd Carrying the Peasant Girl* vase (No. 72) we see how Woodall's great carving skill enabled him to display the human foot beneath rippling water (Fig. 28). On the *Iris* vase (No. 73), we note the detail of three fish nibbling at the petals being dropped into the water (Fig. 29). The most amazing detail of all is the small area in front of the face of the central figure of the *Moorish Bathers* (No. 64). The tip of the eyelash of the other eye can be seen projecting in front of the bridge of the nose (Fig. 30)! In the colonnaded area, slightly larger than a square inch, ten meticulously executed columns can be seen. On the floor leading to the doorway at the end of the corridor is a rug with a border design. The door at the end is sufficiently ajar to admit a thin ray of light along its edge! Without magnification, none of this is visible to the human eye.

George Woodall remained at T. Webb & Sons until his retirement in 1911, but he continued to carve masterpieces of cameo glass in his own studio at Kingswinford until his death in 1925. He has left an unmatched heritage of magnificently carved cameo glass. Of all his figural plaques, he selected *The Moorish Bathers* (No. 64) as his masterpiece. Because the figural cameo glass pieces required the greatest technical skill and artistry, they were the acknowledged masterpieces of this art form. If one were to list all the figural pieces carved by all the English cameo glass carvers, then one might begin to understand the extent and the greatness of George

Woodall's output. He alone carved ten times as many figural cameo glass objects as all the others combined.

Woodall increased the speed of his cameo production by the skillful use of the engraving wheel. A foot-operated lathe and as many as fifty copper wheels ranging in size from a pin point to three inches in diameter allowed him to reduce the lengthy time required for the laborious figure carving.

It is known that in cameo carving an artist can modify botanical designs by adding or by substituting a leaf or a petal if some small mishap should produce an unwanted chip. No such leeway is afforded in figural work. Every line must be precise, for a single error can ruin the glass sculpture. Woodall must have used some guide for his consistently elegant work. Despite this, his daughter Alice has commented that as far as she was aware, it was her father's normal practice to draw the final design directly upon the piece he intended to carve. She knew of only one preliminary drawing done for a piece by her father. (No. 149).

Numerous books of engravings with statuary and paintings were available to Woodall. The books he owned and those at Thomas Webb & Sons contained his models. The works of Canova, Flaxman, Wedgwood, Reni, Boucher, and others were his inspiration. Antonio Canova, perhaps more than any other artist, became a source for Woodall's carving. An illustration from one of these books, reproduced here, shows the basis for Woodall's *Dancing Girls* (No. 71, Fig. 33). The figure on the left (Fig. 31) with her hands overhead was engraved by Bertini, entitled *Danseuse*, and was executed for a Russian nobleman. The figure on the right (Fig. 32) with her hands on her hips was engraved by Fontana; it too is named *Danseuse* and was executed for the Empress Josephine. Another source that Woodall utilized for a plaque was a reproduction from the painting of *Diana at the Bath* by François Boucher (Fig. 34)—compare the figural outlines of the painting with Woodall's plaque of *Diana and Nymph* (No. 69). Other examples of Woodall sources can be readily ascertained in the works previously listed. Woodall's *Origin of Painting* is undoubtedly a version of the *Maid of Corinth* by Joseph Wright of Derby.

Fig. 28 Detail of foot, *Shepherd Carrying the Peasant Girl* (No. 72).

Fig. 29 Detail of fish in water, *Iris Vase* (No. 73).

In addition to Northwood's tazzas of Shakespeare, Flaxman, and Newton, there are only eleven English cameo glass portrait medallions known. It is not unexpected that of these, eight were carved by the prolific George Woodall (Nos. 54-57): Lord Kelvin, now in the Royal Society; Mrs. Martin, present location unknown; Judge and Mrs. Winans, Thomas Webb & Sons Museum; the Armenian Girl (No. 54); Gladstone (No. 57); Dr. and Mrs. S. Parkes Cadman (Nos. 55-56), both related to George Woodall through his wife. The other three include the portrait of Joseph Silvers (No. 58) carved by Joshua Hodgetts in 1926, Bismark by F. Kretschman in 1886, and Queen Victoria (No. 59), possibly carved by Kretschman.

Fig. 30 Detail of central figure, *Moorish Bathers*, (No. 64).

Between 1880 and 1890, a change occurred in cameo glassmaking; at Stevens & Williams, production of cameo glass was divided among the designer, the etcher, and the engraver. Preparation of cased glass was still a problem, and accidents in its manufacture were unavoidable. A skilled group of glassmakers worked on blanks with much thinner opal casing. Excess glass could be removed by acid more quickly and easily than by using the engraving wheel, thus facilitating the task of the engraver. Some annealed blanks were sent from Brierley Hill to J. & J. Northwood's Wordsley works for his glass artists and engravers to work upon. The decorator drew the design on the white acid-roughened surface and then filled in the design with a bituminous paint which resisted hydrofluoric acid. The paint was also applied to protect the inside of the object. After drying, all of the unprotected opal of the outer layer was dissolved by a mixture of hydrofluoric and sulphuric acid; when the underlying color of the body was revealed, the acid was washed off with water and the bituminous paint removed with a solvent. The object then went to the engraver. Demand was so great at Stevens & Williams that every available engraver was hired to work overtime and on Saturdays. At Thomas Webb & Sons, the Woodall brothers directed a team of more than seventy engravers who functioned in a similar fashion to produce large quantities of the popular cameo glass. The design books of the Richardson Company illustrate 100 different floral cameo designs which were offered in a variety of colors and shapes. Many of these cameo glass vessels have been attributed to Stevens & Williams and Thomas Webb & Sons. When one also considers the output of other Stourbridge glass companies, one can readily appreciate that hundreds of people were employed in the production of commercial cameo and that thousands of pieces were made.

The variety of articles produced in cameo glass was seemingly endless. Vases and plaques of every size and shape were cased in two to five layers and carved to provide decorative effects. Every form of tableware was duplicated, including complete services. Handles for cutlery, letter openers, button hooks, and place card holders (No. 104) were also made. Scent bottles from small two-inch containers (No. 126) to twelve-inch flasks (No. 122) were made in two and three cased-glass layers; duck heads (No. 121), fish, and dolphins (No. 93) were frequently made as scent bottles. Lighting devices were manufactured in many forms and sizes (No. 135). Oil lamps ranging from eight inches (No. 91) to twenty-three inches in height (No. 90) were exceptionally beautiful and had elaborately cameo-carved bases and shades with matching colored chimneys. Many of these were created by the etchers who produced intricate designs to which a modest amount of carving was added. Etchers became so proficient toward the end of the 19th century that they were able to create elaborate designs in three-layered cased glass (No. 138) and to make complicated outlines for figural pieces (No. 139).

Many ingenious techniques were developed in cameo carving. One unusual approach was *rainbow casing*. It consisted of a single swirled multicolored casing over an opaque white glass base (Nos. 140-141). Sometimes this was done over a specially prepared opalescent glass known as *mother of pearl*. While *rainbow casing* gave the appearance of many different cased layers with a single casing, another technique, *ivory cameo*, eliminated casing altogether. The glass resembled ivory in color and was carved with designs. These elements were highlighted with a brown stain which was fired onto the surface to give the appearance of a patina suggesting age. Some ivory pieces have glass jewels glued onto the surface to further enhance their "precious" appearance.

Chinese and Japanese glass became extremely popular in 19th-century England. Chinese glass and snuff bottles carved in the cameo technique during the Qianlong period (1735-1796) influenced Thomas Webb & Sons very much. Lionel and Daniel Pearce, who worked for Webb, excelled in carving glass in the oriental style. Compare the two snuff bottles (Nos. 82-83) carved by them with some of Chinese manufacture (Nos. 23-27). The Pearces also carved the wonderful two-handled flask (No. 81) in the oriental style. Thomas Webb & Sons produced two- and three-color cameo vessels of more western shape with overall decoration in the same style (Nos. 76 & 134). A vase in the Oriental Collection, Museum of Fine Arts, Boston (No. 86), decorated by the marquetry technique, is almost certainly a product of Thomas Webb & Sons. The colorless body is carved in the English Rock Crystal style with transparent blobs of color applied and carved to highlight the decoration.

Cameo glass plaques were combined with English Rock Crystal carving by the marquetry technique to create a new decorative effect (No. 120). In precise areas on vessels made of colorless glass, plaques of white-on-red cased glass were applied; after cooling, these inserts were cameo-carved. The vessel was then cut, carved, and polished. The result was often striking.

Close inspection of the edge of many of the cameo glass objects reveals an interesting fact. Many have a layer of colorless glass between the colored inner and outer layers (Fig. 35). If the object is made of three colored layers, the colorless layer is often a fourth layer in between the inner colored layer and the two outer colored layers. In the latter instance, the two outer layers are cameo-carved so that one provides background color for the decoration in the other.

Fig. 31-32 *Danseuse*, engravings by Bertini and Fontana after Canova. Photos Dr. Leonard S. Rakow.

54

It is strange that we can find no record of this frequent intervening colorless glass layer. The reason for the layer of colorless glass between the others is quite puzzling. Strangely enough, when this fact was brought to the attention of the various glasshouses in Stourbridge, they were unable to explain its purpose. Our research revealed that this additional colorless layer appeared to be present more often in Thomas Webb & Sons objects than in those from Stevens & Williams, but with so many unmarked cameo glass artifacts made in similar shapes by different Stourbridge glasshouses, it could have been done by others as well. We feel that this colorless glass layer was probably included between the colored layers to provide some leeway during the acid removal of the outer layer. By its use, the excess outer layer could be removed entirely without accidentally removing part of the inner colored layer and thus changing its even coloring. Other possibilities for its use may be to avoid accidentally thinning of the base layer during the course of carving the outer layer; to provide body for the glass when the inside and outside colored layers are thin; or to utilize it as an in-between layer for glasses with disparate coefficients of expansion. We have not noted the existence of this layer in the figural carved cameo pieces, except for the *Aphrodite and Attendants* plaque, by John Northwood II. (No. 43)

The English cameo glass industry was brilliant but short-lived. Its history can be divided roughly into three periods. The first period was from 1875 to 1880 when the first pieces were carved with hand tools; the engraving wheel had only a subordinate role. One individual did the designing and the carving from beginning to end, and some of the greatest pieces were done during this period under Northwood, Richardson, Locke, and Lechevrel. George Woodall, along with a handful of others such as John Northwood II, William Northwood, James Hill, and Jim Millward, maintained the superlative quality of this type of cameo glass carving until his death in 1925.

Fig. 33 *Dancers Vase* (No. 71), England, Stourbridge, late 19th-early 20th century, Thomas Webb & Sons, George Woodall.

The second period of cameo glass manufacture was from 1880 to 1890. A considerable market for cameo glass had developed, especially in America. The early hand-carved pieces were too costly, too time-consuming, and too few to meet the popular demand. Stevens & Williams, Thomas Webb & Sons, and the Richardson Company responded to this market by producing "commercial" cameo glass, which was less detailed and less expensive.

In the third period, beginning by 1889, the popularity of cameo glass suddenly declined. Despite all the attempts to reduce its cost, prices remained high, and much cheap imitation cameo glass was made during this period. Imitation cameo was frequently made by using thin opal-cased glass with a printed pattern of acid-resist ink so that a short acid immersion produced a shallow opal relief on a colored ground. This crude imitation debased all cameo glass. Other cheaper cameo glass imitations, mostly from the Continent, were produced by painting and firing white enamel onto colored glass. By 1900, as the general public lost interest, the production of cameo glass had practically ceased.

Very little carved cameo glass was made in America, although many patents were registered for manufacturing cameo glass by etching, pressing, gluing, molding, and other time-saving methods without actually carving it. Gillinder & Sons produced a few cameo vases (Nos. 142-144) about 1880. These remained with family members until recently when they were given to the Smithsonian Institution.

Fig. 34 *Diana at the Bath*, oil on canvas, François Boucher (1703-1770). Photo The Louvre, Paris.

They are not very delicate; the cased layers are quite thick, and the details of the carving are rather flat. This is the sort of work one would expect from an initial effort.

There is, however, one exception: Louis Comfort Tiffany, profoundly affected by the work of Emile Gallé which he saw at the World Exhibition in Paris in 1889, produced some completely cased and truly cameo-carved vases (No. 145). The cameo-carved and marquetry-decorated objects he and Gallé made inspired imitations in the Art Nouveau style decorated by acid-cutting alone. Although many companies in Europe and America supplied this commercial market, the cost of cameo carving remained exorbitant.

In 1933, the Libbey Glass Company made a dozen cameo goblets. Each goblet (No. 146) had four panels, each cameo-cut with white-on-ruby on clear glass, with two Trojan heads and two classic female heads, and each goblet required eighty hours of copper-wheel engraving time.

Even today, the casing and carving of cameo glass commercially is precluded by the cost and the great amount of time required. Its beauty, however, constantly challenges glass craftsmen. Among the notable contemporary American glassmakers who are making cameo glass are Max Roland Erlacher and Douglas Beck Merritt.* Erlacher, of Corning, New York, formerly chief engraver at Steuben, works with copper engraving wheels on cased blanks blown by Charles Lotton. Merritt, with his associate Barry Sautner of Vandermark-Merritt, Flemington, New Jersey, cases his own glass and has developed a sandblasting technique for removing the excess colored glass.

Erlacher, born July 11, 1933, in Innsbruck, Austria, graduated from the Glasfachschule Kramsach where he studied with Master Engraver, Herman Schiller. He then worked at J. & L. Lobmeyr under Stefan Rath, and during his fourth year there he received his Master Certification degree. In 1957 he emigrated to the United States and engraved glass at Steuben Glass in Corning, New York. Today Erlacher engraves glass in his own studio and recently has devoted much of his time to perfecting cameo glass carving.

Fig. 35 Detail of colorless layer separating colored layers (No. 97).

Merritt, born July 5, 1951, in the United States, graduated from Leas McCrae College in 1971. He apprenticed with Jerry Vandermark of the Jamestown, Virginia, Glass House, and now heads the Vandermark/Merritt Glass Studio. He makes and blows his own glass as well as decorating it. He has devised a new method of carving cameo glass and has developed fine sandblasting instruments. Sautner, who served his apprenticeship with Merritt six years ago, has spent the last three years perfecting his expertise in this special field.

There is an extraordinary history behind the production of cameo glass. After an eighty year period of decline, cameo glass may again have an exciting future.

L.S.R. and J.K.R.

*Unfortunately, the objects made by these two glass artists had not been finished at press time; we were unable to include them in the catalog, but they can be seen in the exhibition.

36. *Milton Vase*
England, Wordsley, 1878, John Northwood I

Left
35. *Portland Vase*
England, Wordsley, 1876. John Northwood I

39, 38, 37. *Three Tazzas: Newton, Shakespeare, Flaxman*
England, Wordsley, about 1880, John Northwood

40. *Shakespeare Tazza*
England, Wordsley, about 1877, attributed to
John Northwood

41. *Pegasus Vase*
England, Wordsley, 1892, John Northwood

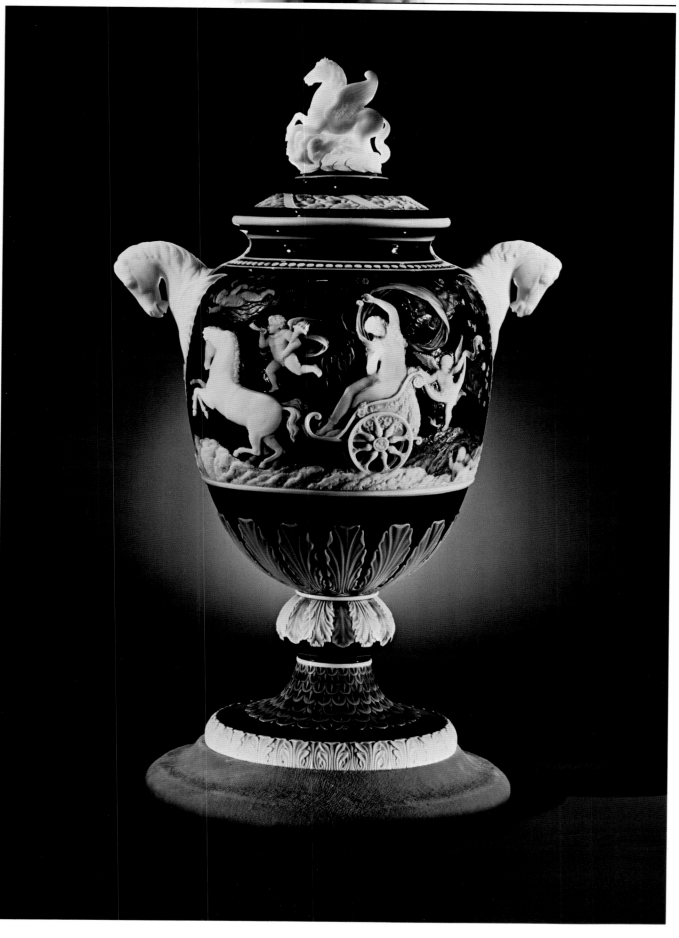

42. Plaque, *Venus Instructing Cupid*
England, Stourbridge, about 1895,
William Northwood

44. Plaque, knight fighting the devil
England, probably Wordsley, 1880,
attributed to James Benjamin Hill

43. Plaque, *Aphrodite and Attendants*
England, Wordsley, about 1906, John Northwood II

45. Vase, *Venus Arising from the Sea*
England, Stourbridge, about 1878, Alphonse Lechevrel,
George Woodall

46. Vase, *Birth of Venus*
England, Stourbridge, about 1878, Alphonse Lechevrel,
George Woodall

47. Portland Vase
England, Wordsley, 1878, Joseph Locke

49. Plaque, *The Immortality of the Arts*
England, Brierley Hill, 1887, Frederick Carder, Stevens & Williams

50. Vase with Fish
England, Amblecote, late 19th century, attributed to Stevens & Williams, Frederick Carder design

48. Vase, *Cupid Sailing on a Cockle Shell*
England, Wordsley, 1878, Joseph Locke, Hodgetts, Richardson and Co.

51. Plaque, *The Boxing Day Meet*
England, Stourbridge, about 1885, H. J.
Boam, Thomas Webb & Sons

52. Plaque, nymph in a crescent moon
England, probably Amblecote, about 1888, attributed to Ludwig Kny

55, 56. Portrait med-
allions, Dr. and Mrs.
Samuel Parkes Cadman
England, Amblecote,
about 1895, George
Woodall

57. Portrait medallion, Gladstone
England, Stourbridge, early 20th century,
George Woodall

54. Portrait medallion, *Armenian Girl*
England, early 20th century, George Woodall

59. Portrait medallion, Queen Victoria
England, late 19th century

58. Portrait plaque, Joseph Silvers
England, Amblecote, 1926, Joshua Hodgetts,
Stevens & Williams

61. Vase with two handles
England, Amblecote, late 19th century, Woodall team, Thomas Webb & Sons

60. *The Great Tazza*
England, Amblecote, about 1895, Woodall
team, Thomas Webb & Sons

63. Plaque, *Venus and Cupid*
England, Stourbridge, about 1890, George Woodall

62. Plaque, *The Attack*
England, Amblecote, about 1900, Thomas and George Woodall

64. Plaque, *Moorish Bathers*
England, Amblecote, 1898, George Woodall

74

67. *Muses Vase*
England, Amblecote, about 1885, Thomas and
George Woodall, Thomas Webb & Sons

66. Vase, *Antarctic*
England, Stourbridge, late 19th century, George Woodall

65. Ginger Jar
England, Stourbridge, late 19th century, Thomas Webb & Sons

68. Plaque, *Aphrodite*
England, Amblecote, 1892, George Woodall,
Thomas Webb & Sons

69. Plaque, *Diana and Nymph Bathing*
England, Amblecote, 1878, George Woodall

70. Plaque, *Andromache*
England, 1902, George Woodall

71. Vase, *Dancing Girls*
England, Amblecote, about 1880-1885, George Woodall,
Thomas Webb & Sons

72. Vase, *Shepherd Boy Helping Peasant Girl across Stream*
England, Amblecote, late 19th century, George Woodall, Thomas Webb & Sons

73. *Iris Vase*
England, Amblecote, about 1880, George Woodall, Thomas Webb & Sons

75. Vase, *Before the Race*
England, Stourbridge, late 19th century,
Thomas and George Woodall, Thomas Webb
& Sons

74. *Cleopatra Vase*
England, Amblecote, 1896, Thomas Webb &
Sons, George Woodall

77. Vase, floral design, gilt
England, Amblecote, 1885, Thomas Webb &
Sons

76. Lamp base, tricolor
England, Amblecote, about 1890, probably
Woodall team, Thomas Webb & Sons

78, 79, 80. Three enameled cameo vessels
England, Amblecote, or Stourbridge, about 1890, Thomas Webb & Sons; enameling (No. 78) by J. Kretschman, all probably gilt by Jules Barbe

84. Vase, oriental style
England, Stourbridge,
late 19th century, at-
tributed to F. Kretsch-
man, Thomas Webb &
Sons

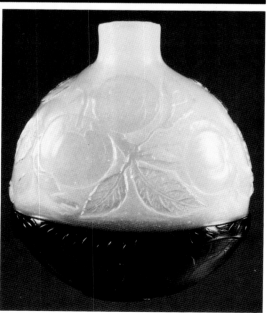

82. Snuff Bottle
England, Amblecote,
about 1890, Thomas
Webb & Sons

83. Snuff Bottle
England, Amblecote,
1890

Opposite
81. Canteen vase,
oriental style
England, Amblecote,
about 1890, Thomas
Webb & Sons

85. Vase, *Boy in a Tree*
England, Stourbridge, late 19th century

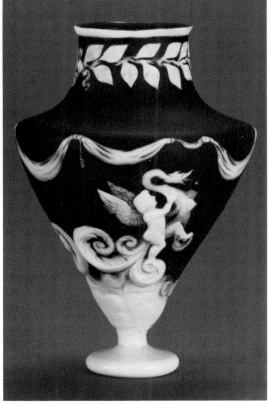

86. Vase, marquetry with birds and fish
England, 19th century, probably Thomas
Webb & Sons

88. Vase with classical motifs
Italy, Venice, 1878

89. Amphora
Italy, Venice, late 19th century

87. Bottle, *Moore Vase*
Italy, Venice, late 19th century

90, 91. Two lamps
England, late 19th century

95-100. Two- and three-color cameo vessels
England, late 19th century

101-107. Two- and three-color cameo vessels England, late 19th century

108-114. Two- and three-color cameo vessels
England, late 19th century

Opposite
Top Right
92-94. Apple vase, scent bottle, and decanter
England, about 1885

115-120. Two- and three-color cameo vessels
Europe and England, late 19th century

121-127. Cameo scent bottles and miniatures
England, late 19th century

128-133. Two- and three-color cameo vessels
England, late 19th century

134-137. Two- and three-color cameo vessels
England, late 19th century

138-141. Acid-etched and rainbow-cased glass
England, late 19th century

144. Vase, maple leaf design
Philadelphia, 1880-1890, James Gillinder

143. Vase, elm leaf design
Philadelphia, 1880-1890, probably James
Gillinder

Top Left
142. Vase, maple leaf design
Philadelphia, 1880-1890, possibly James
Gillinder

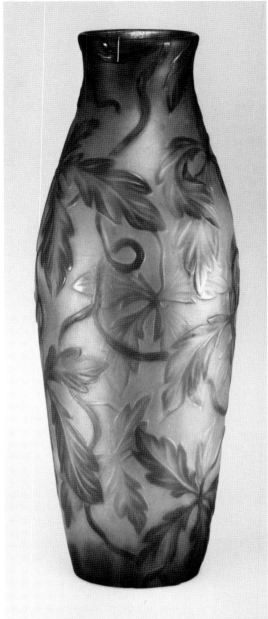

145. Vase, leaves and vines
New York, Corona, L.I., 1900-1920, Louis C.
Tiffany; marked "9911A," signed "L.C. Tif-
fany Favrile"

146. Chalice, *Victoria* pattern
Toledo, Ohio, 1933, Libbey Glass Company

149. Drawing for *Cleopatra* plaque England, Amblecote, about 1880, George Woodall

147. Lagynos (unfinished)
Eastern Mediterranean, Hellenistic, late 3rd-1st century B.C.

148. Beaker (unfinished blank)
Islamic, 9th-10th century, probably Iran, Nishapur

93

152. Blank, for a Portland vase
England, Wordsley, 1878, Hodgett's, Richardson and Co.

150. Vase, *Cupid and Psyche*
England, Stourbridge, 1889, Frederick Carder

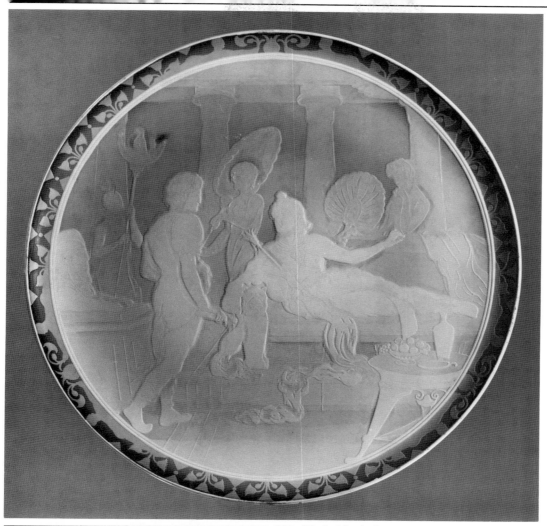

153. Unfinished plaque, *Antony and Cleopatra*
England, Amblecote, about 1895

154. Vase, *Solitude*
England, probably Wordsley, 1918, J. B. Hill

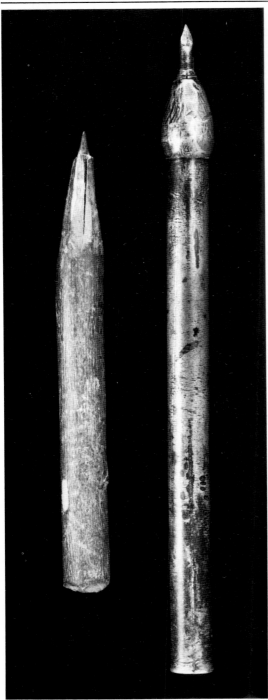

155, 156. Carving tools
England, early 20th century

157. Vase, unfinished
England, Stourbridge, 1932, Joshua Hodgetts

1 Augustus and Roma

Rome (?), early Imperial, first quarter of the 1st century A.D.

H. 11 cm; W. 10 cm
Kunsthistorisches Museum, Vienna (IXa 59)

Brown and white banded chalcedony; cameo carved. A youthful, lightly-bearded Augustus, partially draped and crowned with a laurel wreath, sits on an elaborate throne and turns his head toward Roma, seated next to him. He supports a double cornucopia with his right hand and holds a long scepter in the left. Roma, fully draped, wears a plumed helmet pushed back on her head. She holds a shield in her right hand and gestures toward the Emperor with her left. This is a fragment of a larger cameo which probably had additional figures. The gilt and enameled mounting was added in the early 17th century.

Although the composition of the figures is similar to those on the *Gemma Augustea* (Fig. 1), the modeling differs. The figures are well-carved but appear less tightly composed, perhaps because they are part of a fragment. A strong Hellenistic tradition is apparent in the style. Since it is a fragment, the iconography is difficult to interpret, but some indication of the Augustan peace and its welcome prosperity for the Roman Empire must surely be part of the correct interpretation.

Simon, *Portlandvase*, p. 44, pl. 13.1; W. Technau, *Die Kunst der Römer* (Geschichte der Kunst, Altertum II 1940) p. 113, fig. 86; F. Eichler and E. Kris, *Die Kameen Im Kunsthistorischen Museum*, (Publikationen aus der Kunsthistorischen Sammlungen in Wien, Band II), Vienna, 1927, pp. 51-52, no. 6, pl. 3, for extensive bibliography.

2 Tiberius

Rome, possibly carved by Herophilus, Early Imperial, second quarter of the first century A.D.

H. 13.8 cm; W. 7.8 cm; reconstructed diam. 16 cm
Kunsthistorisches Museum, Vienna (IXa 61)

Brown and white banded onyx; cameo-carved in three layers. A youthful, lightly-bearded Tiberius, wearing a heavily decorated cuirass and crowned with laurel, faces right. A mantle is draped over the cuirass and is secured on the left shoulder with a sliding brooch.

The (roughly) circular gem originally must have had a second figure, probably the mother of Tiberius, Livia, facing the Emperor. The *aegis*, a goatskin often decorated with a Gorgon's head and bordered with snakes, is an attribute of Athena. It is difficult to tell whether it is a separate attribute here or merely part of the cuirass decoration. Similarity of hair treatment on a signed turquoise glass gem carved by Herophilus suggests that he also may have carved this gem.

Eichler and Kris, *op. cit.*, p. 59, no. 13, pl. 6; for Herophilus gem, *ibid.*, pp. 58-59, no. 12, pl. 6.

3 The Morgan Cup

Late Hellenistic or Early Roman, said to have been found at Herakleia in Pontus, on what is now the southern Turkish coast of the Black Sea, second half of the 1st century B.C.

H. 6.2 cm; D. 7.6 cm
The Corning Museum of Glass (52.1.93) Gift of Arthur A. Houghton, Jr. Ex coll: J. Pierpont Morgan, J. Durighello

Opaque white over translucent deep blue glass; blown and cameo-carved. Some patches of iridescence over surface, one crack originating at the rim and running down in a J-shaped curve. The central scene, defined by two horizontal lines, is interpreted as a Dionysiac ritual. A young woman, praying for fertility, comes to the sacred precinct and makes an offering before a herm of Silenus. She has tethered her donkey to a tree and is assisted by two maidens and a satyr. One of the women brings offerings while the other reveals the holy snake in the covered box. The satyr prepares a covering where the woman will sleep and be visited by the snake. Carved on the concave base is an eight-petaled rosette surrounded by two concentric white rings which form a thin base ring to protect the decoration.

The Morgan Cup is the earliest fully preserved cameo glass of Roman date known. It relates more to Hellenistic gem carving in style than to the controlled Neoclassicism of the Augustan period. Although an Alexandrian source has been suggested for this cup, craftsmen may have moved from Alexandria to Rome in order to be near the most profitable market. The cup was sold in Paris in 1912 and remained in the J. P. Morgan Collection until it was purchased for The Corning Museum of Glass.

Charleston, *Masterpieces* p. 35, no. 9; *Short History*, p. 26, fig. 17; *Guide*, p. 15, no. 8; I. Jucker, "Hahnenopfer aus einem Späthellenistischen Relief," *Archaeologischer Anzeiger* 1980, Heft 3, pp. 445-446, figs. 6-8; Simon, *JGS* 6, pp. 14-21, see footnote 4 for earlier bibliography, fig. 2 for a drawing of the scene by Miss Suzanne E. Chapman.

4 Bottle

Roman, possibly made in Alexandria; said to have been found near Eskischehir, Turkey, last quarter of the 1st centruy B.C., first quarter of the 1st century A.D.

H. 7.6 cm

Kofler-Truniger Collection, Lucerne

Opaque white over deep blue glass; blown and cameo-carved. Some incrustation, pitting and patches of weathering product; handle (?) broken away from rim. The base carved with an elaborate rosette. The body carved with figures which stand on a single thick ground line. To the left, a boy with a garland approaches an Egyptian altar; in the center, a boy with a fluttering mantle raises a curved rod or stick in front of a second altar with a fire burning on top. To the right of this altar is a statue of an Egyptian pharaoh holding a crook in his right hand and an offering jar in his left. He wears a double crown, lappet wig, pleated kilt, and stands in front of an obelisk inscribed with nonsense hieroglyphs; behind the obelisk is a gnarled tree.

The shape of the vessel and the iconography of the scene are unusual. The stylization of the Egyptian elements and the nonsense hier-

oglyphs make it difficult to accept an Alexandrian origin; compare the quality of carving with the Egyptian scene on the Corning fragment (No. 9). The side of the first altar base is carved with an ibis; a baboon crowned with a sun disc sits on the top. The second altar, with fire burning on top, is dedicated to Isis; a Uraeus crowned with a sun disc is carved on the side. The hieroglyphs carved on the obelisk and its sockel seem to be a conglomeration of pharaohs' names, but they are unreadable. Jucker suggests the scene depicts Horus, son of Isis, paying homage to his mother and to the sun god, Amon-Re, here represented as a pharaoh. The base rosette and its surrounding leaves are extremely well-modeled and are far more realistically executed than the rosette on the base of the Morgan Cup (No. 3).

Kunstmuseum Luzern, p. 72, illustration on p. 32; H. Jucker, "Promenade archaeologique durch die Austellung der Sammlung Kofler in Kunsthaus Zürich," *Antike Kunst* 8, 1965, pp. 40-55; *JGS* 4, 1962, p. 140, no. 5.

5 Portland Vase disc

Rome (?), Early Imperial, first half of the 1st century A.D.

D. 12.1 cm

The British Museum, London (G.R. Dept. Gem 4036)

Opaque white over translucent deep blue glass; cameo-carved, recut into a disc from a larger plaque. A young man in an Asiatic costume and Phrygian cap tilts his head forward and raises his right index finger to his chin. A bough with large leaves fills the area above and behind him.

The figure is generally identified as Paris, the son of Priam, King of the Trojans. Hind, however, has suggested this figure may be the young Iulus, son of Aeneas, ancestor to the Julio-Claudian Emperors. The gesture, used to express doubt or perplexity in classical art, suggests that the scene depicted is the famous Judgement of Paris. Paris was chosen to select the most beautiful goddess among Hera, Athena, and Aphrodite. Aphrodite, bribing Paris by promising him the most beautiful woman in the world as a wife, won the golden apple inscribed "to the fairest." The apple had precipitated the contest when it was tossed among the guests by Eris (Strife) at the wedding of

Peleus and Thetis. Paris's subsequent abduction of Helen, the most beautiful among mortals, was the cause of the Trojan war.

The disc was obviously cut from a larger plaque since the figure and the foliage are both trimmed in an arbitrary fashion. The colors of the glasses differ from those of the Portland and the disc is a less "saturated" blue. Scholars generally believe that the original Portland was an amphora with a pointed base, not unlike the Naples Vase from Pompeii (Fig. 7). The disc has a groove cut through the iridescence on the undecorated side, suggesting that it was added recently to the Portland. Nonetheless, it is difficult to explain the iconographic coincidence of Paris on the base and the marriage of Peleus and Thetis on the sides of the Portland itself if the repair were recent. Were fragments of Roman cameo glass of such size available in the early 16th century, when the vase was discovered?

Although we are not proposing the original Portland was designed *with* this disc, there are two Roman *lagynoi*, both in the Corning Museum, with technically related bases. Each vessel has a disc base which fits into a carefully finished groove and was presumably affixed with a resin. It is noteworthy that one of the vessels is an unfinished cameo blank (No. 147). Considering these vessels and their curious construction, the possibility of Roman repair for the Portland Vase may be more reasonable.

Hind, "Portland Vase", p. 25; Haynes, pp. 13-14, 24-26, pl. 9a; *Masterpieces*, p. 46, no. 54.

6 The Auldjo Jug

Roman, from Pompeii, Early Imperial, late second or third quarter of the 1st century A.D.

H. (inc. handle) 22.8 cm
The British Museum, London (59.2-16.1). Ex. coll: R. Auldjo

Opaque white over deep blue glass, appearing black; blown and cameo-carved. Broken and restored. The shoulder is decorated with an "inhabited" vine scroll. The body is covered with an elaborate grape and ivy tendril.

The Auldjo Jug and the famous Naples Vase (Fig. 7) were excavated at Pompeii in 1834

from the Casa di Goethe. The style of the foliage is closely related; Haynes suggests that they were perhaps carved by the same person. Many of the cameo fragments which preserve only foliate decoration compare closely with the Auldjo jug.

Haynes, p. 23, pl. 13; Simon, *Portlandvase*, p. 47, pl. 24.2; Kisa, p. 584, fig. 190; Eisen, p. 157, fig. 111.

7 Cup or skyphos (fragment)

Roman, first quarter of the 1st century A.D.

H. 4.9 cm
The Corning Museum of Glass (66.1.57). Ex coll: G. Sangiorgi

Opaque white over translucent deep blue glass; blown and cameo-carved. Fragment of vessel wall, no rim or base profile preserved. Surface covered with several rows of garlands; birds peck at fruit and leaves.

This fragment most closely relates to the elaborate decorative motifs usually reserved for decoration on silver vessels or relief sculpture. The swags and garlands on the silver skyphos from Hildesheim and the Julio-Claudian funerary altars seem to be the closest parallels. The height of the relief is notable, even when compared with the garlands on the Naples Vase (Fig. 7). The bird on the Corning fragment stands in the round, its head completely separated from the background by undercutting.

Previously unpublished. For references on the Hildesheim silver, see p. 9, footnote 11; D. E. Strong, *Roman Imperial Sculpture*, London, 1961, p. 94, fig. 58, the altar of Memmius Ianuarius (30 A.D.) in the Ny Carlsberg Glyptotek, Copenhagen, is one of a large class of such monuments datable to the first half of the 1st century A.D. His altar has fruit and birds similar to the Corning fragment.

8 Six-layered cup (fragment)

Roman, first half of the 1st century A.D.

H. 5.9 cm; W. 6.6 cm
The Corning Museum of Glass (62.1.24a). Ex. coll: G. Sangiorgi

Translucent amethyst, green, and opaque white over translucent dark blue glass; blown and cameo-carved. Two joining fragments preserve the rim and body of a cup decorated with a young man standing before a drape hung across some trees. Behind the drape, a woman extends a *kyathos* or ladle in her right hand.

The scene is similar to that on the Morgan Cup, where the satyr extends a drape to shelter a portion of the sacred precinct. The male figure extends his right arm while holding another drape or mantle over his left arm. Although he is not a satyr, he wears a fillet of grapes and grape leaves. The scene may be another preparation for a "divine" visitation, as that depicted on the Morgan Cup. A non-joining fragment which is decorated with the head of a woman in front of a billowing drape, probably belongs to the same cup. Brill has studied the fragment and observed that the orientation of the interior polishing groove indicates that the figure of the woman was in a reclining or stooping position. Thus, she may be the woman who seeks the blessing of the sanctuary.

These fragments are extraordinary not only for the excellence of carving but for the remarkable sequence of layers. On the translucent deep blue matrix, the following layers have been applied: opaque white, translucent amethyst or red, translucent green, opaque white, translucent green, and translucent amethyst or red. The entire thickness of the fragment is just over three millimeters; the blue layer is less than 1.5 mm thick, the casing layers range from 0.20 to 0.50 mm. The sequence of the layers on the non-joining fragment is the same, as are the layer thicknesses. Brill has noted that the amethyst or red layer has an opaque red layer with a turbid purple or amethyst layer beneath. More study will be required to determine if these two colors were exploited separately in the carving. We do not know if this stratification was intentional. The fillet in the man's hair suggests an amethyst color was intended: the grapes were cut from this layer; the leaves were cut from the green layer. Obviously, the thickness of the translucent layers would affect the color intensity. Weathering layers make certain identification impossible, but the figure is white and stands in front of an amethyst drape. The drape over his arm is green but is carved close to the white layer. The designs on the stretched drape are white while the tree behind is amethyst and green.

These fragments are presently the most sophisticated examples of the cameo carver's art known. No other fragments are known with such complex layering sequence and delicate modeling.

Short History p. 26, fig. 18; *Guide*, p. 15, no. 9; *JGS* 5, 1963, p. 141, no. 4.

9 Amphoriskos (fragment)

Roman, possibly Alexandria, late 1st century B.C. - early 1st century A.D.

H. 5 cm; D. (shoulder) 4.6 cm
The Corning Museum of Glass (66.1.63). Ex. coll: G. Sangiorgi

Opaque white over translucent deep blue glass; blown and cameo-carved. Dull surface, iridescent weathering film. The handles, cut from opaque white trails, were applied and cut after the vesel was blown; they are not cut from the cased layer. The shoulder preserves the heads of two Egyptians carrying animals over their shoulders.

The proportions of the amphoriskos suggest a miniature version of the Naples Vase (Fig. 7). The two men walk in opposite directions, each carrying an animal over his shoulder. The man walking to the left holds a young gazelle or antelope which seems to be trying to jump free. The less well preserved figure on the right carries a ram(?) with a long tail. The work is unlike that on other fragments with Egyptian processions or offerings. The fragments in Karlsrühe or London do not exhibit the same control of detailed surface decoration and precision. Although the carving quality is closely related to the Egyptian style, it is difficult to assign it to an Alexandrian workshop on this basis alone.

Previously unpublished. For Karlsrühe and London fragments, see Simon, *Portlandvase*, pl. 14.1 and 3; *Vatican Cat.*, p. 36, no. 331, pl. 1.

10 Plaque (fragment)

Rome (?), Early Imperial, Claudian (?), mid-first century A.D.

H. 4.8 cm; W. 6.9 cm
The Corning Museum of Glass (59.1.110). Ex. coll: R. Smith

Opaque white on deep amethyst glass; cameo carved, pitted with iridescent film over most of the figure. Portion of the legs and torso of a draped figure holding the legs of a small animal in his right hand.

A satyr, servant of Dionysos, brings an offering to the god's precinct. The large size of the fragment and the broad treatment of the carving make it an interesting comparison with Nos. 14 and 15.

Simon, *JGS* 6, pp. 27-29, fig. 20; Simon, *Portlandvase*, p. 78, pl. 15.1; *Smith Cat.*, p. 105, no. 183; Musée de Mariemont, *Catalogue des Verres Antiques de la collection Ray Winfield Smith 8 mai - 15 septembre 1954*, Bruxelles, 1954, p. 16, no. 41.

11 Cup or skyphos (fragment)

Roman, first half of 1st century A.D.

H. 7.8 cm; W. 8.8 cm
The Metropolitan Museum of Art, New York (16.174.47). Rogers Fund purchase

Opaque white over translucent deep blue glass, blown and cameo-carved. Fragment preserves the rim and vessel wall of a deep cup or skyphos with a thin iridescent film flaking away from a pitted surface. The carved scene is a pastoral landscape with sinuous pine trees and a rustic altar. A draped female statue holding a jug stands on a rocky outcrop, and, immediately in front, a goat suckles a kid. A satyr with a short mantle draped around his neck turns back to look at the animals and raises a stick in his right hand.

The delicate modeling and the interrelationship of the various figures on this piece are extraordinary. The wand or branch and the wind-tossed hair of the satyr relate to the boy with a similar stick and flowing mantle on the Egyptian-style bottle (No. 4). The rocky outcrop on which the statue stands is similar to the rocky outcrops on the Portland Vase (Fig. 5). The scene must depict an offering or visitation at a Dionysiac shrine.

Simon, *Portlandvase*, p. 52, pl. 16.4; R. W. Smith, "The Significance of Roman Glass," *MMA Bulletin* 8, no. 2, Oct. 1949, p. 60, illus; *MMA Bulletin* 18, 1923, p. 127, fig. 7.

12 Oval platter (fragment)

Roman, said to have been found near the villa of Tiberius on Capri, first half of the 1st century A.D.

L. 51.9 cm; H. 24.1 cm

The Metropolitan Museum of Art, New York (81.10.347). Gift of Henry G. Marquand, 1892

Opaque white over amethyst glass; cast, cameo-carved. Broken into six large pieces and repaired; weathering product of mottled brown over parts of surface give the impression of several colored glass layers. Within the oval plaque, profiled at the lip by three concentric rings, are several mollusks, a crab, and a squid (?).

This fragment seems to have been part of a huge platter or perhaps a tabletop. Pliny's description of a gaming table made from a gemstone which was carried in Pompey's Triumph (see p. 8) seems less astonishing given such fragments of cameo glass as this. The subject is related to mosaic glass inlays of fish or mosaic floors decorated with food.

These subjects would be appropriate for a dining room; presumably all of the creatures swimming or crawling about the cameo platter were edible types.

Simon, *Portlandvase*, p. 52, pl. 14.4; R. W. Smith, "The Significance of Roman Glass", *MMA Bulletin* 8, no. 2, Oct. 1949, p. 60 (illus.).

13 Plate or plaque (fragment)

Roman, Imperial, Flavian (?), third quarter of the 1st century A.D.

H. 16.8 cm
The Metropolitan Museum of Art, New York (17.194.358). Gift of J. Pierpont Morgan; Ex coll: J. Greau.

Opaque white over translucent deep blue glass; cast or blown and cameo-carved. Fragment preserves a central design of the chariot of Aphrodite rising from the sea.

The elaborate parade chariot rises from the sea drawn by putti. Only the legs of one figure are preserved, another rises from the sea alongside the group. The scene is bordered by a stylized bead and reel band. The bold and elaborate quality of the chariot suggests the somewhat later date for the figural carving.

Greau Cat., p. 83, no. 582, pl. 61; W. Froehner, *La Verrerie antique déscription de la Collection Charvet*, Paris, 1879, p. 85, note 5; for a related wheel, see F. Fremersdorf, *Römisches Buntglas in Köln*, Die Denkmäler des römisches Köln, 3, Köln, 1958, p. 22, pl. 6, bottom.

14 Large plaque (fragment)

Roman, first half of the 1st century A.D.

H. 15.3 cm; W. 13.3 cm; Th. 1.5 cm
The Corning Museum of Glass (66.1.60). Ex coll: G. Sangiorgi.

Opaque white over translucent deep amethyst glass; cast and cameo-carved. Broken on all sides, thick white weathering crust over entire surface. Fragment preserves part of a helmet; above it, a device decorated with two heraldic winged griffins. The helmet rests on some drapery(?).

The elaborate shield or crest may be part of the helmet. All may be part of a trophy, a monument of captured arms erected at a battleground. A similar trophy is being raised in the lower register of the *Gemma Augustea* (Fig. 1).

Previously unpublished.

15 Plaque (fragment)

Roman, mid-first century A.D.

H. 10.1 cm; W. 14 cm; Th. 1.2 cm
The Corning Museum of Glass (72.1.12). Ex coll: R. Smith, Norton, J. Greau

Opaque white over translucent amethyst glass. Cast and cameo-carved. Broken on all sides, brilliant iridescence. Fragment preserves a thick base line with portion of a footstool and a *kline* or couch with a long cloth draped over it.

Although the base glass is similar to the other plaque fragment (No. 14), the carving style on this fragment is bolder and less delicate. The turned legs of the *kline* are typical of wood, ivory, and metal couches of the early 1st century A.D. The lion-leg stool appears to have a cushion on the top.

Greau Cat., p. 66, pl. 50, no. 7.

16 Skyphos

Roman, said to have been found in a Parthian tomb in Iran, last quarter of the 1st century B.C.-1st quarter of the 1st century A.D.

H. (preserved) 9.7 cm; D. 10.4 cm; estimated length across handles, 18 cm
Private Collection, New York

Opaque white over translucent deep blue glass; blown and cameo-carved. Thick dark weathering crust flaking away to reveal bright iridescence, some pitting; broken and repaired, foot broken in antiquity. Two scenes depicted on a thick white groundline. On one side, a partially draped woman reclines on a rocky outcrop as she is served by a maidservant on the right; a satyr with a *syrinx* or pan-pipe and a crooked staff turns to observe them. The other side features another satyr playing a lyre in front of a woman, seated beside a tall stele and holding a small cup. The satyr turns away from the seated woman to observe a second woman leaning on a krater and drinking from a large bowl.

The skyphos is said to be one of a pair found in a Parthian nobleman's tomb. The style of the carving moves from sure and competent treatment of drapery and musculature to strange elongation and exaggerated proportion. It is difficult to suggest it is a provincial work, given the numerous elements which relate it to many other Roman cameos including the Portland. The most immediate similarity is the pose of the central figure to that of Thetis or Helen and Aphrodite, the reclining and seated figures on the Portland. The figure on the skyphos appears to be hybrid, with the stiff supporting left arm of the seated Aphrodite on the Portland, but the right arm is bent over the head as the reclining Thetis or Helen. The rocky outcrop is similar to the Portland ledge as is the drapery. Here the satyr stands off to the side with the same isolation and reserve as the figure of Poseidon or Nereus does on the Portland. Both the skyphos satyr and the Portland sea god are framed by trees in a similar fashion. The satyr holds a crooked staff similar to one being tied to the tree on the Besançon pitcher (No. 17) and the Metropolitan fragment (No. 11). On the second side, the young woman drinks from a shallow bowl like that on the Besançon pitcher and leans on a krater more elegantly profiled and rendered in more correct perspective than that of the Morgan Cup (No. 3). The seated lady, firmly planted on a rock outcrop reminiscent of the Portland, holds a cup which is the shape of the Morgan and sits beside a tall stele like those of the Portland and the Besançon pitcher.

The details of the stele are difficult to see; there is a seated figure, but certainly not a Papposilenus or Priapus herm. The figure appears fully draped and seems to wear a helmet. Beneath the handles are carved elaborate heads of Papposilenus. The heads are not at all goat-like, thus eliminating a parallel with the Pan heads on the Portland. Viewing the cup from the "ends," the design seems to run from the handle between the standing satyr on the first side and the seated lady on the second side. Turning the cup to the other handle, the maidservant on the first side and the woman drinking by the *krater* are placed under the trees at rather strange angles. It is as if the carver ran out of space. There is still much research to be done on this skyphos.

Previously unpublished.

17 Pitcher or trefoil jug

Roman, from Besançon, third quarter of the 1st century A.D.

H. (preserved) 14 cm; reconstructed H. 23 cm
Musée des Beaux Arts, Besançon, France

Opaque white over deep blue glass appearing black; blown and cameo-carved. The upper portion of neck, rim, and handle lost; two large sections of the body and two-thirds of the base missing; dull pitted surface. The base of the handle is decorated with a Gorgon mask, the hair tied in a Heracles knot beneath the chin. To the right of a stele, a woman with torch and *thyrsus* and a satyr prepare to make an offering at a table laden with vessels. The satyr is tying a shepherd's crook to the pine tree behind the table. The two scenes are linked together by the *thyrsus* which the draped woman holds or rests against the stele of Ariadne (?); the *thyrsus* touches the head of Papposilenus. The action to the left of the stele takes place around a herm of Papposilenus. He is draped, and holds a horn symbolizing fertility in his right hand. In front of the herm, an older satyr laps wine from a drinking bowl and drunkenly snaps his fingers, almost ignoring his impatient son who is eager to share the drink. The scene takes place on a thick rocky baseline divided into three narrow strata.

The jug was excavated near the Gallo-Roman cemetery of Besançon in 1886. Simon has pointed out the similarity of the foliage on this vessel to that of the Morgan Cup, and the shape of the cup from which the satyr drinks his wine is a larger version of the Morgan. The Besançon pitcher is stylistically different from other cameo vessels, and the glass itself is different in surface and feel. The pitcher may be a local Gallo-Roman product rather than an imported object brought to the area by a Roman general in charge of the local garrison.

Simon, *JGS* 6, pp. 24-26, figs. 14-16; M. Dayet, "Une Scene des Mystères de Dionysos sur une vase en verre a deux couches", *Revue Archéologique de l'Est* I, 1951, pp. 40-43, pl. 4; A. Vaissier and A. Caston, "Le Vase Priapique en verre du Musée de Besançon" *Memoires de la Société d'Emmulation de Doubs* 6, Series 1, 1886, pp. 249-254, and separate plate

18 Hunting bowl

Late Roman, from a cemetery at Stein am Rhein-Burg, second half of the 4th century A.D.

H. 6.2 cm; D. 22.2 cm
Museum zu Allerheiligen, Schaffhausen, Switzerland (23096)

Translucent amethyst over colorless glass with a greenish tinge; blown and cameo-cut. Slight iridescence; broken and repaired; some restoration. A hunter in a short *Chlamys* or tunic lunges with a spear toward a springing panther. The hunter, panther, and a stylized tree all rest on a simple wide groundline; an inscription ΠΙ EZH CAIC (ΠIE ZACAIC) "Drink and Live" forms an outer border. Below, on a second groundline, a hunter with a spear fights a bear. Behind the bear lies a shield and stylized palm branches, behind the hunter, a quiver and palm branch.

The inscription, "Drink and Live," is a typical late Roman salutation, as is the bowl's subject matter and style. However, it is fascinating to note that the highly stylized tree can still be identified as a pine and retains a broken lower branch so typical of the same trees depicted on earlier Roman cameos. It is a remarkable link between the cameo tradition of Imperial Rome and the Islamic cameo tradition. The color combination and the flatter cameo cutting suggest a strong link not only with the famous *diatreta* of the 4th century but with later Islamic cameo glass which also emphasized outline rather than modeling. The scene takes place not in the woods but in an amphitheater. The hunters or *Venatio* pursue the animals amid prizes and good luck palm branches tossed down from the fans. The small circular blobs with crosshatched lines represent silver bowls and plates tossed from the stands. Such items can be seen on ivory diptychs of the same period. The Schaffhausen bowl is a vital addition to the history of glass and the understanding of the cameo technique.

Paris, L'Orangerie du Luxembourg, *A l'Aube de la France. La Gaule de Constantin à childeric*, Paris, 1981, no. 379; H. Urner-Astholz, "Zu Werkstall und Bildschmuck der römischen Jagdschale von Stein am Rhein", *Schaffhauser Beiträge zur Geschichte* 53, 1976, pp. 108-121; W. U. Guyan, "Stein am Rhein, Kelten-Römer-Germanen, *Helvetia Archaeologica* 6, 1975, pp. 38-77; H. Urner-Astholz, "Die römische Jagdschale und Eine Kugelschliffschale von Stein am Rhein", *Schaffhauser Beiträge zur Geschichte* 51, 1974, pp. 7-61; W. U. Guyan, *Erforschte Vergangenheit II: Schaffhauser Frühgeshichte*, Schaffhausen, 1971, pp. 53-62

19 Cup with gazelles

Islamic, said to have been found at Nishapur, Iran, mid-10th Century

H. 8.5 cm; D. 8.6 cm
L. A. Mayer Memorial Institute for Islamic Art, Jerusalem (G24)

Translucent turquoise-green over colorless glass; blown and cameo-cut. Iridescent film over surface; broken and repaired, some restoration. Three gazelles with long horns and elongated bodies walk beneath a stylized Kufic inscription; rim and base decorated with horizontal bands.

The thin outline of the relief cutting, the stylization of the figure and the infilling of the body with a drilled dot motif point to a mid-10th century date for the manufacture. Compare this vessel with the eagle and gazelle ewer (Fig. 13) and the Corning jug (No. 21).

R. Hasson, *Early Islamic Glass*, Jerusalem 1979, p. 16, fig. 25 and cover; S. Nardi, et al., *L. A. Mayer Memorial Institute of Islamic Art*, Jerusalem, 1976, (n.p.) fig. 10; *JGS* 18, 1976, p. 240, no. 8.

20 Cup with stylized tree

Islamic, Iran (?), late 9th-10th century

H. 8.7 cm; D. 9.6 cm
The Chrysler Museum of Art, Norfolk, Virginia (68.6). Gift of Walter P. Chrysler

Transparent emerald green over colorless glass; blown in an open mold, applied wide marquetry bands, wheel-cut. Patches of thick dark and iridescent weathering crust on surface; broken and repaired. Two bold stylized tree motifs decorate the vessel walls.

This type of cylindrical cup is the most frequently preserved Islamic form to be decorated by the marquetry technique. It is probable that the green layers of these vessels were applied in limited areas so that less glass had to be removed. This technique is really marquetry work, rather than the true cameo technique which was used in making the gazelle cup (No. 19) where a colorless cup was cased completely with turquoise green glass.

Previously unpublished.

21 Jug or pitcher (fragments)

Islamic, said to be from Iran, late 10th century

H. 17 cm; D. (body) 11 cm
The Corning Museum of Glass (59.1.489). Ex. coll: R. Smith

Translucent, dark green over colorless glass; blown in a mold and cameo-cut; wide-mouthed jug with an elaborate openwork handle. On the neck are two heraldic animals with horns, long tails, and open mouths. On the horizontal shoulder are two snakes face to face; the edge of the shoulder and the base are decorated with openwork ovals alternating with circles. The cylindrical body has two running split hooved and horned(?) animals with birds perched on their backs. The animals on the neck and body are infilled with drilled dots, the underside is decorated with two concentric circles.

The casing and many stylistic elements link this object to the gazelle and eagle ewer (Fig. 13). The way in which the neck register is framed, the decorative surface treatment of the figural outlines, and the stylized flourishes or tails are all similar. It is difficult to believe the same cutter was responsible, but the jug and ewer might have been made in the same workshop. The stylistic elements have been extensively discussed by Oliver. The snakes on the shoulder are related to the one on an amethyst relief-cut plate in the Corning Museum (55.1.139), although the rest of the relief cutting differs markedly. The form, the treatment of the figures by drilling, and the raised oval and circular border patterns suggest a date in the late 10th or early 11th century.

Oliver, *JGS* 3, pp. 22-23, figs. 23-24; *Smith Cat.*, p. 263, no. 530, pl. 11, for the amethyst relief-cut plate.

22 Ginger Jar

Chinese, 1736-1795, Qianlong mark

H. 19 cm
Dr. and Mrs. P. H. Plesch Collection

Translucent deep red over colorless glass which has the appearance of crushed ice; blown and cameo-carved. Body decorated with a garden setting in which children play around a pavillion and bridge. Cover has a band of playing children; an openwork carved pagoda serves as a finial.

A typical color combination is used on a form which is usually decorated with geometric or simple floral designs. The combination of openwork carving and high relief is exceptional.

Plesch, "Chinese Glass", p. 77, fig. 14; A. von Saldern, *Meisterwerke der Glaskunst aus internationalem Privatbesitz*, Düsseldorf, 1968, p. 121, no. 350.

23 Snuff Bottle

Chinese, Yangzhou, 1830-1900

H. 6.6 cm
Marian Swayze Mayer Collection (608)

Opaque orange brown over opaque white glass; blown and cameo-carved. Carnelian stopper. Carved delicate floral sprigs with flowers, butterflies, spiders, bats, and birds. Maker's seal on side.

This type of bottle is often called a *seal type* or *seal school* because the maker's seal is incorpo-

rated in the decoration. The names are usually fanciful but may be useful in the future for attributing such pieces to specific workshops and craftsmen.

Moss. *Glass Snuff Bottles*, no. 84.

24 Snuff Bottle

Chinese, 1780-1880

H. 7.1 cm
Marian Swayze Mayer Collection (751)

Opaque pink over black glass; blown and cameo-carved. Nephrite stopper. Decorations are the eight Buddhist symbols.

The color combination is notable; black glass was uncommon and usually employed as a casing on poorer quality bottles in the 19th century.

Moss, *Glass Snuff Bottles*; no. 72.

25 Snuff Bottle

Chinese, 1820-1900

H. 7.8 cm
Marian Swayze Mayer Collection (282)

Translucent green over opaque pink over opaque white; blown and cameo-carved. Rose quartz stopper. Landscape with birds and lotus plants.

The stylized leaf motif on the neck is similar to that on the Norfolk bottle, No. 29.

Previously unpublished.

26 Snuff Bottle

Chinese, Yangzhou, 1850-1920

H. 6.4 cm
Marian Swayze Mayer Collection (261)

Opaque red brown over opaque yellow. Amethyst stopper. Fruit harvest scene in a rocky landscape. Opposite side has monkeys frolicking in a tree.

The scene is reminiscent of the oriental-style gourd vase, No. 85, probably made by Thomas Webb & Sons.

Moss, *Glass Snuff Bottles*, no. 83.

27 Snuff Bottle

Chinese, 1720-1850

H. 6.7 cm.
The Corning Museum of Glass (81.6.6). Gift of Marian Swayze Mayer (546)

Opaque deep blue over opaque deep green; blown and cameo-carved. Rose quartz and jade(?) stopper. Horned dragons undulate over the surface.

Moss, *Glass Snuff Bottles*, no. 2.

28 Hookah Base or vase

Chinese, 1768-1769

H. 15.2 cm
Museum and Art Gallery, City of Bristol (N4788). Bequest of H. F. Burrows Abbey, The National Art-Collections Fund, 1950

Opaque white over translucent pinkish red with colorless base and rim; blown and cameo-cut. Squat body decorated with bats in cloud scrolls, lotus petals on base. Cut into base in Arabic *1172*, gilt.

The color combination is unique in known Chinese glass; the translucent red has a slight dichroic effect when viewed alternately in transmitted and reflected light. The colorless rim and base are curious. They seem to be fused to the vessel although it has been suggested that they are rock crystal. If this is the case, some type of adhesive would be necessary, but none is visible

Simon Digby, "A Corpus of 'Mughal' Glass," *Bulletin of the School of Oriental and African Studies*, 36, Part I, 1973, p. 85, pls. 1, 2.

29 Bottle

Chinese, 18th century, probably Qianlong (1735-1796)

H. 2.2 cm
Chrysler Museum, Norfolk Virginia (76.1). Gift of Walter P. Chrysler

Opaque light green over opaque white with yellow, blue, and pink marquetry appliqués; blown, cameo-carved and marquetry technique. Bottle decorated with overall floral design highlighted by marquetry appliqués.

Previously unpublished.

30 Vase in the form of a fish

Chinese, 18th century, probably Qianlong (1736-1795)

H. 17.9 cm
Museum of Fine Arts, Boston (11.9759)

Opaque medium deep blue over opaque white. Blown and cameo-carved. Scales are cut into the white glass.

The color combination is striking and the form is unusual.

Previously unpublished.

31 Rouge box

Chinese, 18th century, probably Qianlong (1736-1795

D. 2.7 cm
Museum of Fine Arts, Boston (11.9778)

Translucent red over opaque white glass; opaque yellowish-green glass base; blown or cast and cameo-carved. Flat domed cover decorated with a floral motif and dragonfly. Base carved into a stylized floral form.

Previously unpublished.

32 Bottle

Chinese, 18th century, probably Qianlong (1735-1796)

H. 23.1 cm
Museum and Art Gallery, City of Bristol (N4650). Bequest of H. F. Burrows Abbey, The National Art-Collections Fund, 1950

Translucent red over colorless glass which has the appearance of crushed ice; blown and cameo-carved. Neck decorated with a dragon in lotus scrolls; body has four panels of peach, pine, prunus, and bamboo with birds, bats, and deer.

Although the color combination of red over white glass is commonly used in Chinese cameo glass, the overall intricacy of the carving is unusual. Peter Hardie, Curator of Oriental Art at the Bristol Museum, has suggested a close affinity to Chinese lacquer work. This stylistic relation with another material may imply an early Qianlong date.

Royal Academy, London, *International Exhibition of Chinese Art*, London 1935/6, p. 247, no. 2750.

33 Pot

Chinese, 18th century, probably Qianlong (1735-1796)

H. 5 cm
Museum and Art Gallery, City of Bristol (N4565). Bequest of H. F. Burrows Abbey, The National Art-Collections Fund, 1950

Opaque green over deep blue glass; blown and cameo-carved. The globular form seems to represent an eggplant. Carved wooden lid.

Previously unpublished.

34 The Warrior Vase

China, 18th century, probably Qianlong, 1735-1796

H. 48.9 cm
The Corning Museum of Glass (57.6.10). Gift of Benjamin D. Bernstein.

Translucent red over colorless glass having the appearance of crushed ice, blown in a mold and cameo-carved. The globular body is decorated with five galloping horsemen. One brandishes a pair of lances while the rest carry large globular bags (?) on shorter handles. The action takes place in a rocky landscape dotted with trees and bushes. A ramp leads to an elaborate temple carved on the neck; four monks (?) on the porch of the temple point to a hanging painted scroll decorated with a headless figure.

The size and quality of carving on this vase are extraordinary. It would appear that some sort of tournament is depicted. The objects which have been described as racket or fan-shaped seem to be bulbous rather than flat. They resemble punching bags in that they appear to be segments of cloth or leather sewn together. Whether they are targets for the lancer or oversize padded maces used to unseat him is unclear.

Charleston, *Masterpieces*, p. 180, no. 82; *Short History*, p. 34, no. 28; Warren, "Chinese Glass," p. 114, fig. 40; *Guide*, p. 80, no. 104.

35 Portland Vase

England, Wordsley, 1876, John Northwood; signed "J. Northwood 1876"

H. 25 cm
Collection of Dr. and Mrs. Leonard S. Rakow

Opal over transparent deep blue glass; acid-dipped and cameo-carved.

First replica in glass of the Portland Vase, blank made at Pargeter's Red House Glassworks. Northwood spent three years carving his vase. For a discussion of the original Portland see p. 13. Northwood's piece broke when almost completed and was glued together. When Frederick Carder was taken to see this vase by his father, he decided to work in glass rather than pottery (see p. 49).

Corning, *English Cameo Exhibition*, fig. 4; Wakefield, *Nineteenth Century British Glass*, pp. 42-43; George Savage, *Glass and Glassware*, pp. 24-25; D. R. Gutterey, *From Broad Glass to Cut Crystal*, pls. 64, 65; John Northwood II, "The Reproduction of the Portland Vase," 1924, vol. 8. Rakow, Leonard S. and Juliette K. "The Glass Replicas of the Portland Vase." *Journal of Glass Studies* 24, 1982 (in press).

36 Milton Vase

England, Wordsley, 1878, John Northwood; signed "John Northwood 1878"

H. 33 cm
Collection of Mr. and Mrs. Billy Hitt; Ex coll: Pargeter family

Opaque white on transparent deep blue; acid-dipped and cameo-carved. Decorated on one side with Archangel Michael entering the Garden of Eden; on the other are Adam and Eve. Adam amid tropical plants and flowers, points to the angel.

Commissioned by Philip Pargeter, inspired by John Milton's "Paradise Lost."

John Northwood, pp. 43-44, illus. p. 52; *Cameo Glass*, pp. 20-21, illus. p. 98, pl. 2, fig. 5.

37 Flaxman tazza

England, Wordsley, 1880, John Northwood; signed "J. N. 1880"

D. 23.5 cm
Collection of Dr. and Mrs. Leonard S. Rakow;
Ex coll: Pargeter family

Opaque white over transparent deep blue glass; acid-dipped and cameo-carved.

Profile bust surrounded by a dot border, rim decorated with a border of white holly leaves and flowers. This tazza was made to honor John Flaxman, noted English sculptor, and Wedgwood's jasperware medallion of Flaxman was used as the model for the portrait. Flaxman is supposed to have made the self-portrait for Wedgwood while in Italy between 1787 and 1794.

Reilly, Robin and Savage, George. *Wedgwood. The Portrait Medallions.* London: Barrie and Jenkins, 1973, p. 138-g. *John Northwood*, pp. 44, 53; Beard, *Cameo Glass*, pp. 21, 101.

38 Shakespeare tazza

England, Wordsley, 1880, John Northwood

D. 23.5 cm
Collection of Dr. and Mrs. Leonard S. Rakow;
Ex coll: Pargeter family

Opaque white over transparent deep blue glass; acid-dipped and cameo-carved.

Profile bust surrounded by a dot border, rim decorated with a border of oak leaves and acorns. Unsigned, although both the Flaxman and Newton tazzas (Nos. 37, 39) are signed. The three tazzas were commissioned by Pargeter. The profile bust of William Shakespeare was presumably copied from Wedgwood's jasperware medallion, modeled by William Hackwood. Both heads show a small earring in the left ear.

Reilly and Savage. *Wedgwood. The Portrait Medallions*, p. 303—a; Beard, *Cameo Glass*, pp. 21, 101.

39 Newton tazza

England, Wordsley, 1878, John Northwood; signed "J. Northwood 1878"

D. 23.5 cm
Collection of Dr. and Mrs. Leonard S. Rakow;
Ex coll: Pargeter family

Opaque white over transparent dark blue glass; acid-dipped and cameo-carved. Profile surrounded by a dot border, rim decorated with a border of ivy and berries.

Wedgwood's jasper medallion of Newton was the model for Northwood; he even repeated the background star.

Reilly and Savage, *Wedgwood. The Portrait Medallions*, p. 258-c; Beard, *Nineteenth Century Cameo Glass*, pp. 21, 101; *John Northwood*, pp. 44, 53.

40 *Shakespeare Tazza*

England, Wordsley, about 1877, attributed to John Northwood

D. 23.2 cm, H. 9.6 cm
Collection of Dr. and Mrs. Leonard S. Rakow

White opal over transparent dark blue; acid-dipped and cameo-carved. Profile of Shakespeare in a circle of white dots. Rim decorated with a circle of laurel leaves and berries. Broken and restored with a new foot; apparently a duplicate of Shakespeare tazza on a stand (No. 38).

This recently discovered tazza has not been listed among John Northwood I's works, but it has been authenticated by his grandson, Kenneth Northwood. There are minor differences between this head and the signed Shakespeare Tazza (No. 38). Both have been copied from Wedgwood's jasperware medallion.

Previously unpublished.

41 *Pegasus Vase*

England, Wordsley, 1882, John Northwood; signed "J. Northwood 1882" on body and cover

H. 53.5 cm
Smithsonian Institution, The National
Museum of American Art, Gellatly Collection

Opaque white glass over translucent dark blue; acid-dipped and cameo-carved. Three parts—the flanged foot, the ovoid body with horsehead handles and the domed cover with an opal finial of Pegasus. On the front, Aurora, goddess of the dawn, rides her chariot with attendants. Amphitrite, wife of Neptune and goddess of the sea, in a shell drawn by seahorses on the reverse. Intaglio-carved cupids decorate the dark blue ground.

Amphitrite is often incorrectly identified as Aphrodite. Commissioned by Mr. Wilkes Webb, the *Pegasus*, (or Dennis) *Vase* was the largest and last of Northwood's pieces. In Paris, at the Exhibition of 1878, still unfinished, the vase won the Gold Medal. It took Northwood more than two years to complete the vase which was sold to Tiffany & Co. in New York.

John Northwood, pp. 44-46 (illus), p. 54; Beard, *Nineteenth Century Cameo Glass*, pp. 22-24 (illus), Frontispiece.

42 Plaque, *Venus Instructing Cupid*

England, Stourbridge, about 1895, William Northwood; signed "W. Northwood"
D. 29.6 cm
Collection of Dr. and Mrs. Leonard S. Rakow

Opaque white over frosted deep amethyst glass; acid-dipped and cameo-carved.

The plaque was sent to Canada during World War II for safekeeping.

Beard, *Cameo Glass*, p. 29.

43 Plaque, *Aphrodite and Attendants*

England, Wordsley, about 1906, John Northwood II
D. 38.7 cm
Collection of Dr. and Mrs. Leonard S. Rakow

Opaque white over colorless on transparent flashed deep red glass; acid-dipped and cameo-carved.

Central composition of Aphrodite on a shell surrounded by attendants. Eros above, two cupids riding "dolphins" in front, sea nymph on a rearing hippocamp, another on a triton; a second triton blowing on a conch.

The design was selected by John Northwood I, adapted from an illustrated plate in a German folio. John Northwood II began work on the plaque when he was about seventeen years old, stopped after eighteen months of work, and did not resume work on it until after the death of his father, John Northwood I, in 1902. Completed four years later, it fell from a table and broke. It was displayed in the showroom of Stevens & Williams after being pieced together again.

Service, John H. "George Woodall and His Work." *American Pottery Gazette*, Jan. 1906, p. 23; Turner, *Trans Soc. Glass Tech*, 8, 1924, pp. 92T-93T; Revi, *Nineteenth Century Glass*, 1967 ed., p. 141 (illus).

44 Plaque, knight fighting the devil

England, probably Wordsley, 1880; attributed to James Benjamin Hill
D. 29.9 cm
Collection of Dr. and Mrs. Leonard S. Rakow; Ex coll: James T. Hill, Jr., grandson of J.B. Hill

Opaque white over frosted light blue glass; acid-dipped, cameo-carved, and unfinished. A knight in armor fighting the devil.

Hill was a designer, decorator, and etcher at Stevens & Williams where this plaque was probably made.

Beard, *Cameo Glass*, p. 30; *John Northwood*, pp. 10, 62, 79.

45 Vase, *Venus Arising from the Sea*

England, Stourbridge, about 1878, Alphonse Lechevrel, George Woodall; signed "Geo. Woodall and Alphonse Lechevrel"
H. 20 cm
Broadfield House Glass Museum, Dudley

White opal over transparent deep blue glass; acid-dipped and cameo-carved. Reworked, handles removed, overall surface polished.

One of a pair of vases (No. 46) made for Benjamin Richardson and exhibited at the Paris Exhibition in 1878. After the vases remained unsold for a long time, George Woodall was commissioned to rework some of the carving, remove the handles and Lechevrel's signature. Presumably Woodall's signature would improve the "quality" of the vases. One Lechevrel signature still remains.

46 Vase, *Birth of Venus*

England, Stourbridge, about 1878, Alphonse Lechevrel, George Woodall; signed "Geo. Woodall" on waves, "The Birth of Venus" on base
H. 28.5 cm
Collection of Dr. and Mrs. Leonard S. Rakow

White opal over transparent deep blue glass; acid-dipped and cameo-carved. Reworked, handles removed, matt-surface where design was reworked.

One of a pair (No. 45) made for Benjamin Richardson and exhibited at the Paris Exhibition of 1878. At Richardson's invitation, Lechevrel came from France to train apprentices in cameo carving. When the vases remained unsold for a long time, Woodall was commissioned to rework and sign them, perhaps as late as 1923. Lechevrel's signature, "AL 1877", was ground off this vase, but part of his initials can be detected near a crack which can be seen in several original photographs.

Beard, *Cameo Glass*, pp. 55-57, p. 132, fig. 72, 73, and 75; Michael Braby, "Rivalling the Romans," *Art and Antiques*, Sept. 6, 1975, p. 27; Revi, *Nineteenth Century Glass*, pp. 146-148; Corning, *English Cameo Exhibition*, p. 21, no. 2.

47 Portland Vase

England, Wordsley, 1878; signed "Joseph Locke, Wordsley 1878"
H. 25 cm
Collection of Dr. and Mrs. Leonard S. Rakow

Opaque white over translucent dark blue glass; acid-dipped and cameo-carved.

Replica of the Portland Vase commissioned by Benjamin Richardson and exhibited at the Paris Exposition in 1878, although Locke had

not finished thinning his figures at the time of the exhibition. The vase was unfinished because Locke, after a disagreement with Richardson, left his employ and emigrated to the United States.

Revi, *Nineteenth Century Glass*, p. 150; Beard, *Antiques*; pp. 472-474; Corning, *English Cameo Exhibition*, no. 5, p. 24.

48 Vase, *Cupid Sailing On a Cockle Shell*

England, Wordsley, 1878, Hodgetts, Richardson and Co., Joseph Locke
H. about 23 cm
Collection of Mr. Horace Richardson

Opaque white over yellow-brown glass; acid-dipped and cameo-carved.

This vase was recently located by the Rakows on a research trip to England in December 1981. Photographs of other Locke pieces exist but have not been located to date.

Beard, *Cameo Glass*, p. 61, fig. 86.

49 Plaque, *The Immortality of the Arts*

England, Brierley Hill, 1887, Frederick Carder, Stevens & Williams
D. 33 cm
The Corning Museum of Glass (69.2.39).
Ex coll: Frederick Carder

Opaque white over translucent amber glass; acid-dipped and cameo-carved. Unfinished, central group after La Mercie.

Published photographs often show Frederick Carder working on this piece.

Beard, *Nineteenth Century Glass*, pl. 21, fig. 81; Corning, *English Cameo Exhibition*, p. 20, no. 2; Gardner, *Frederick Carder*, p. 8, ill. 16, colorplate I.

50 Vase with fish

England, Amblecote, late 19th century; attributed to Stevens & Williams, Frederick Carder design

H. 30 cm
The Chrysler Museum, Norfolk, Virginia.
Gift of Walter P. Chrysler

Opaque white over frosted colorless on flashed amethyst glass with interior yellow stain (?); acid-dipped and cameo-carved. "Flying" fish amid stylized scrollwork seaweed.

English Cameo Glass, p. 124, C103.

51 Plaque: *The Boxing Day Meet*

England, Stourbridge, about 1885, signed "H. J. Boam," Thomas Webb & Sons

H. 40.6 cm
Courtesy of Leo Kaplan Antiques

Opaque white, frosted purplish brown glass; acid-dipped and cameo-carved. An equestrian scene depicting five riders, including a woman riding sidesaddle and one rider being thrown, within a geometric border and a broad white rim.

This is the only recorded cameo glass carved by Boam. In transmitted light, the color changes from deep brown to apricot.

English Cameo Glass, p. 302; Beard, *Nineteenth Century Glass*, pl. 80.

52 Plaque, nymph in a crescent moon

England, probably Amblecote, about 1888; attributed to Ludwig Kny

D. 24.4 cm
Collection of Dr. and Mrs. Leonard S. Rakow; Ex coll: Mrs. Ludwig Kny

Opaque white over frosted yellow-green glass; acid dipped and cameo-carved. Saucer-shaped plaque with a nymph reclining on a crescent moon.

Ludwig Kny, son of Frederick E. Kny, apparently never signed his few cameo pieces.

Beard, *Cameo Glass*, pp. 65-66; Revi, *Nineteenth Century Glass*, p. 185.

53 Oval blank (not illustrated)

England, Amblecote, about 1880

H. 15.3 cm, W. 11.2 cm
Collection of Dr. and Mrs. Leonard S. Rakow; Ex coll: Alice Woodall

Opaque white over translucent brown glass.

Unworked blank plaque of same type as those used for Cadman portraits by George Woodall.

54 Portrait medallion, *Armenian Girl*

England, early 20th century, signed "The Armenian Girl, Geo Woodall"

H. about 12 cm
Broadfield House Glass Museum, Dudley

Said to be a portrait of George's daughter Alice.

English Cameo Glass, p. 53.

55-56 Portrait medallions, Dr. and Mrs. Samuel Parkes Cadman

England, Amblecote, about 1895, signed "Geo Woodall"

H. 15.7 cm, W. 11.3 cm
Collection of Dr. and Mrs. Leonard S. Rakow

Opaque white over translucent brownish purple glass; acid-dipped and cameo-carved.

Dr. Cadman was related to George Woodall through his mother, sister to Woodall's wife; his wife was Esther Lillian Wooding. Dr. Cadman, a cleric, migrated to the United States in 1890 and served congregations in Yonkers, Millbrook, and Brooklyn. His radio ministry began in 1923 and continued until his death in 1936. Cadman Plaza and Cadman Memorial Church in Brooklyn are named for him.

Gaines, "Portraits", p. 1171.

57 Portrait medallion, Gladstone

England, Stourbridge, early 20th century, signed "G. Woodall"
D. 6.5 cm
Collection of Mr. and Mrs. Billy Hitt

Opaque white over deep red-brown glass; acid-dipped and cameo-carved. Circular plaque with "William • E • Gladstone" cameo-carved around circumference.

58 Portrait plaque, Joseph Silvers

England, Amblecote, 1926, Stevens & Williams; carved by Joshua Hodgetts
D. 22.1 cm
Royal Brierley Crystal Collection

Opaque white over frosted red glass; acid-dipped and cameo-carved. Seated figure framed in an elaborate floral border.

A plaque made to commemorate the 100th anniversary of the founding of the firm.

Joseph Silvers was the grandfather of Colonel Reginald Silvers Williams-Thomas, currently chairman of the board, Royal Brierley Crystal.

English Cameo Glass, p. 418, C421; *European Art Glass*, p. 31, fig. 54.

59 Portrait medallion, Queen Victoria

England, late 19th century
H. 16.8 cm
The Currier Gallery of Art, Manchester, New Hampshire

Opaque white on frosted colorless on flashed red glass; acid-dipped and cameo-carved.

This portrait appears on several other cameo-carved vessels.

60 *The Great Tazza*

England, Amblecote, about 1895, Woodall team; marked "Thomas Webb & Sons Gem Cameo"
H. 42 cm, D. 47 cm
Collection of Dr. and Mrs. Leonard S. Rakow

Transparent red over opaque white on translucent yellow-green on white on dark green glass; acid-dipped and cameo-carved. Tazza is in two parts. The bowl rests on a brass cylinder inserted in pedestal. Clearance between bowl and pedestal, as well as pedestal base and the surface on which it rests, so both pieces can be rotated and viewed.

Photograph from Woodall's album (fig. 26) shows the Woodall team working on the tazza with a cartoon of the tazza on the wall. Upon completion it was purchased by Thomas Goode & Co.

Frontispiece, *European Art Glass*; Corning, *English Cameo Exhibition*, p. 16, fig. 10; *Country Life*, Nov. 3, 1977, p. 1275.

61 Vase with two handles

England, Amblecote, late 19th century, Woodall team; base impressed "Thomas Webb & Sons/GEM CAMEO"
H. 40.6 cm
Collection of Dr. and Mrs. Henry Blount

Opaque white over frosted deep blue glass; acid-etched and cameo-carved. Winged female figures with acanthus leaf bodies hang garlands on an elaborate urn; overall swags and garland decoration.

Incredibly delicate and intricate carving; this is the vase which George Woodall holds in the group portrait of the Woodall team (Fig. 26) from Alice Woodall's photo album.

62 Plaque, *The Attack*

England, Amblecote, about 1900, signed "T. & G. Woodall"
D. 46 cm
Collection of Mr. and Mrs. Billy Hitt

Opaque white over transparent reddish brown glass; acid-dipped and cameo-carved. Central figure holds a diaphanous drape which is being carried off by two winged cherubs. Elaborate borders encircle the entire plaque.

This plaque shows Woodall's mastery of perspective. The details of the temple and the treatment of wisps of smoke are extraordinary.

An article in *The Lady*, June 15, 1899, mentions that "when the artist had reached the last stage but one in the original specimen, a flaw was discovered in the glass, and the whole of the work, which had occupied him for many months, had to be recommenced on a fresh piece of glass . . ."

Beard, *Cameo Glass*, p. 78, illus. p. 130, fig. 70.

63 Plaque, *Venus and Cupid*

England, Stourbridge, about 1890, signed "Geo. Woodall"

D. 46 cm
The Corning Museum of Glass (65.2.19)

Opaque white over frosted deep amethyst glass; acid-dipped and cameo-carved. Central motif of Venus or a young woman and Cupid at the side of a pool in a pseudo-classical setting; bordered with an elaborate vine scroll and rosette pattern.

Charleston, *Masterpieces*, p. 200, no. 92; *Short History*, p. 78, fig. 75.

64 Plaque, *Moorish Bathers*

England, Amblecote, 1898; signed "Geo. Woodall"

D. 45.8 cm
Collection of Dr. and Mrs. Leonard S. Rakow

Opal over frosted, deep amethyst glass; acid-dipped and cameo-carved.

Seven female figures in Moorish setting. This is the largest number of figures on a Woodall piece. Sold to Lord Brookman upon completion and taken to Australia. It is said that this plaque was the only object saved when his home was destroyed by fire. In an interview in the *County Express* in 1912, Woodall designated this plaque as his masterpiece.

Revi, *Nineteenth Century Glass*, p. 155; Beard, *Cameo Glass*, p. 122, pl. 14, fig. 54; Wakefield, *Nineteenth Century British Glass*, p. 43, pl. 66B.

65 Ginger jar

England, Stourbridge, late 19th century; impressed "Thomas Webb & Sons Gem Cameo"

H. 30.5 cm
Courtesy of Leo Kaplan Antiques

Opaque white over frosted deep brownish purple glass; acid-dipped and cameo-carved. Overall floral Arabesque pattern with floral and geometric borders.

The carving of this vase is of the highest quality. The shape and color of the blank suggest this piece is the work of the Woodall team. Note the applied center of the flower on the cover.

66 Vase, *Antarctic*

England, Stourbridge, late 19th century, by George Woodall; base signed "Antarctic"

H. 41.7 cm
The Chrysler Museum, Norfolk Virginia

Opaque white over frosted yellow-green glass; acid-dipped and cameo-carved. Scene of polar bears, penguins, gulls, and ship amid icebergs and choppy seas. Bronze dolphin base.

An extraordinary treatment of an unusual scene.

European Art Glass, p. 51, figs. 42-43.

67 *Muses Vase*

England, Amblecote, about 1885; base signed "T.&G. Woodall. Des. & Sculpts"; impressed "Thomas Webb & Sons/Gem/Cameo"

H. 19.8 cm
Collection of Dr. and Mrs. Leonard S. Rakow

Opaque white over frosted purplish brown glass; acid-dipped and cameo-carved. Five of the nine Muses: Euterpe (flute playing), Erato (love poetry), Terpsichore (dance and lyric poetry), Clio (history) and Thalia, (Comedy).

George carved the figures and Thomas worked on the decorative borders. Interestingly, several of the Muses are incorrectly identified. Only the *Moorish Bathers* (No. 64) has more figures than this vase.

Guttery, *Broad Glass*, p. 142a; Beard, *Cameo Glass*, p. 86.

68 Plaque, *Aphrodite*

England, Amblecote, 1892; signed "G. Woodall 1892"; base impressed "Thomas Webb & Sons/Gem/Cameo/ Aphrodite."

D. 33.3 cm
Collection of Dr. and Mrs. Leonard S. Rakow

Opaque white over frosted purplish brown glass; acid-dipped and cameo-carved.

The most elaborate of the Aphrodite plaques. Aphrodite amid the waves, three cherubs in cartouches dividing the border of seashells into three sections. The water is chipped so that spray and spume sparkle. An additional impression on the base is a stamped "Webb" in a square surrounded by four half-rosettes.

Revi, *Nineteenth Century Glass*, p. 153; Beard, *Cameo Glass*, p. 18, pl. XII, fig. 48; Corning, *English Cameo Exhibition*, p. 28, no. 10.

69 Plaque, *Diana and Nymph Bathing*

England, Amblecote, 1878, signed "G. Woodall 1878"

D. 25.8 cm
Collection of Dr. and Mrs. Leonard S. Rakow

Opaque white over translucent dark purplish brown glass; acid-dipped and cameo-carved. Two figures at the water's edge, rosette border.

After *Le Bain du Diane*, a painting by François Boucher now in the Louvre, Paris (Fig. 34). The background details in the plaque have been simplified.

Beard, *Cameo Glass*, pp. 82, 113, fig. 33.

70 Plaque, *Andromache*

England, 1902, signed "Geo. Woodall"

H. 31.2 cm
Collection of Dr. and Mrs. Leonard S. Rakow

Opaque white over frosted brown glass; acid-dipped and cameo-carved.

Central figure, framed by columns and entablature, stands near a lighted brazier. In the distance a city and a ship are reflected on the water, examples of Woodall's extraordinary ability to create a feeling of perspective.

English Cameo Glass, p. 166, no. 135.

71 Vase, *Dancing Girls*

England, Amblecote, about 1880-1885, signed "G. Woodall"; base impressed "Thomas Webb & Sons/Gem/Cameo"

H. 33.5 cm
Collection of Dr. and Mrs. Leonard S. Rakow

Opaque white over translucent red on frosted yellow glass; acid-dipped and cameo-carved.

An unusual color combination for a Woodall piece. Dancing figures after the Italian sculptor Antonio Canova, see p. 52.

Beard, *Cameo Glass*, p. 113, pl. 9, fig. 36.

72 Vase, *Shepherd Boy Helping Peasant Girl across Stream*

England, Amblecote, late 19th century, signed "G. Woodall"; base impressed "Thomas Webb & Sons/Gem/Cameo"

H. 30.5 cm
Collection of Dr. and Mrs. Leonard S. Rakow

Opal over deep blue on frosted light blue; acid-dipped and cameo-carved.

Elaborate floral swag on reverse with bird. Note the handling of the boy's foot under water, see Fig. 28.

Auction 4, No. 5, Jan. 1971, p. 62.

73 *Iris Vase*

England, Amblecote, about 1880; signed "Geo Woodall," base impressed "Thomas Webb & Sons/Gem/Cameo."

H. 27.3 cm
Collection of Dr. & Mrs. Leonard S. Rakow

Opaque white over frosted purplish brown glass; acid-dipped and cameo-carved. Two-handled vase with female figure dropping petals into a pool. Three fish nibble at the falling petals (Fig. 29).

An excellent example of Woodall's great ability to show underwater objects. An additional impression on the base is a stamp, "Webb," in a square surrounded by four half-rosettes.

"Modern Ceramic Art," *Connoisseur*, Dec. 1907 p. 3, illustrated.

74 *Cleopatra Vase*

England, Amblecote, 1896, signed "Geo. Woodall"; base impressed "Thomas Webb & Sons/Gem/Cameo/ W2848 Cleopatra"

H. 27.5 cm
The Corning Museum of Glass (81.2.27).
Ex coll: Dr. and Mrs. Leonard S. Rakow

Opaque white over frosted purplish-brown; acid-dipped and cameo-carved.

Cleopatra stands in front of an elaborately carved Egyptian temple wall holding a sistrum (musical instrument) in her right hand. Neck and base decorated with stylized papyrus and lotus. Elaborate rosette and papyrus design on reverse.

75 Vase, *Before the Race*

England, Stourbridge, late 19th century, attributed to Thomas and George Woodall; impressed "Thomas Webb & Sons/Gem/Cameo"

H. 30.5 cm
Courtesy of Leo Kaplan Antiques

Opaque white over frosted dark brown glass; acid-dipped and cameo-carved. Three horses and their jockeys with floral and geometric borders.

Very fine carving in low relief; the figures in this vase are reminiscent of the paintings of George Stubbs, particularly the anatomy of the horses. Although unsigned, this vase is listed in the Woodall design book along with a signed version, #W2043.

English Cameo Glass, p. 57; Beard, *Nineteenth Century Glass*, p. 79.

76 Lamp base, tricolor

England, Amblecote, about 1890, probably by the Woodall team, base ring impressed "Thos. Webb & Sons/ Cameo"

H. 45.9 cm
Collection of Dr. and Mrs. Leonard S. Rakow

Opaque yellow over white on frosted purplish brown glass; acid-dipped and cameo-carved. Pear-shaped lamp base open at the bottom, decorated with an overall Chinese floral and geometric pattern including the symbol for "Long Life and Happiness."

The style is similar to the *Great Tazza* (No. 60). This base or one similar was illustrated in the photograph of Thomas Goode & Co's shop in 1891 (Fig. 27).

Country Life, 162, no. 4192, Nov. 3, 1977, p. 1275.

77 Vase, floral design, gilt

England, Amblecote, 1885, Thomas Webb & Sons

H. 27.4 cm
Collection of Dr. and Mrs. Leonard S. Rakow

Opaque white over transparent red on colorless on flashed yellow on opaque white glass; acid-dipped, cameo-carved, and gilt.

Ferns, gilt and grass by Jules Barbe. Yellow ground pales toward the bottom.

Woodward, *Art, Feat and Mystery*, p. 36.

78 Vase, gourd-shaped

England, Amblecote, 1888, J. Kretschman, gilt by Jules Barbe; base impressed "Thomas Webb & Sons/ Gem/Cameo"

H. 22.9 cm
Collection of Dr. and Mrs. Leonard S. Rakow

Opaque white over frosted red glass; acid-dipped and cameo-carved, enameled and gilt.

Oriental-style decoration of carved and enameled gourd vines and dragonflies. Overall background is stipple-gilt. The design is copied from a Chinese snuff bottle.

Keyes, Homer Eaton, "Cameo Glass," *Antiques* 30, no. 3, Sept. 1936, pp. 109-112, (illus); "A Nineteenth-century Masterpiece in Cameo Glass," *Antiques* 28, no. 1, July 1935.

79 Bowl, with cherries, leaves, and butterflies

England, Stourbridge, about 1890

D. 10 cm, H. 10 cm
Collection of Dr. and Mrs. Leonard S. Rakow

Transparent red over frosted greenish yellow glass; acid-dipped, cameo-carved, enameled, and gilt.

The design is probably by Ferreday. The body is enameled by Jules Barbe with green scrolls; leaves, stems, and butterflies are gilt; base decorated with gilt rosette.

Beard, *Cameo Glass*, pl. 20, fig. 79, for similar pattern.

80 Scent bottle

England, Stourbridge, late 19th century, attributed to Thomas Webb & Sons.

H. 7.2 cm
Collection of Susan Kaplan

Opaque white over greenish brown glass; acid-dipped and cameo-carved, enameled and gilt. Decorated with spotted pears and purple plums with deeply veined stems and leaves against a gilt scrollwork background.

English Cameo Glass, pl. C210.

81 Canteen vase, oriental style

England, Amblecote, about 1890; impressed "Tiffany & Co., Paris Exhibition, Thomas Webb & Sons/Gem/Cameo"

H. 20.7 cm
Collection of Dr. and Mrs. Leonard S. Rakow

Transparent deep red over opaque white glass; acid-dipped and cameo-carved. Stylized serpent and octopus amid Chinese clouds and rocky landscape.

Possibly designed and carved by Lionel Pearce.

82 Snuff bottle

England, Amblecote, about 1890, Thomas Webb & Sons

H. 6.1 cm
Collection of Dr. and Mrs. Leonard S. Rakow; Ex coll: Daughter of Lionel Pearce

Opaque white over frosted yellow on opaque white with applied translucent green glass; acid-dipped and cameo-carved.

Flattened and rounded form with a short cylindrical neck. Sides depressed, leaf or base of flower and stems applied on one side and carved; white "petals" have been carved from the white cased layer.

Designed and executed by Lionel and Daniel Pearce.

Beard, *Cameo Glass*, pp. 66-67, illus. p. 142, fig. 94, top row center; *European Art Glass*, p. 29.

83 Snuff bottle

England, Amblecote, 1890

H. 7.6 cm
Collection of Dr. and Mrs. Leonard S. Rakow; Ex coll: Lionel and Dorothy Pearce

Translucent deep blue over opalescent glass; acid-dipped and carved. Grapes and peaches carved in the opalescent layer, overall leaf pattern in the blue layer.

When some of the Pearce bottles were sold, among them were several Chinese bottles which had been used for study. These, too, were sold as Webb cameo glass snuff bottles. Although this bottle is not truly cameo-carved, it was originally illustrated as being made in the Chinese style by Lionel and Daniel Pearce.

Beard, *Cameo Glass*, p. 66-67, illus. p. 142, fig. 94, last bottle bottom row; *European Art Glass*, p. 29.

84 Vase, oriental style

England, Stourbridge, late 19th century, attributed to F. Kretschman; impressed "Thomas Webb & Sons/Gem/Cameo"
H. 14.5 cm
Courtesy of Leo Kaplan Antiques

Opaque white over red on frosted colorless on flashed yellow on opaque white glass; acid-dipped, cameo-carved with appliqués and inlays. Chinese interior with a man seated in front of a mirror; the reverse with flowering peach branches.

The use of appliqués and inlays is unusual and represents a "puddingstone" vase. Among the inlays are a mirror with the man's reflection engraved on it, and *mother-of-pearl* teapot, spider, butterfly, and bird tail. The thick colorless glass between the colored overlays and the white interior give the piece a translucent quality. The vase design appears in the Woodall design book, number K107, execution by F. Kretschman.

Beard, *Nineteenth Century Glass*, pp. 65, 66; *English Cameo Glass*, p. 335.

85 Vase, *Boy in a Tree*

England, Stourbridge, late 19th century
H. 20.7 cm
Collection of Dr. and Mrs. Leonard S. Rakow

Opaque ivory over translucent red glass; acid-dipped and cameo-carved.

Unusual carving on a double gourd shape. Oriental style, with man and woman picking coconuts in a tree, monkey near the top, birds, flowers, and other foliage. The extensive use of deep undercutting is unique, the work of a master. Paper label on base, "Phillips of Mount Street London." The piece was acquired with an invitation to visit Phillips to see George Woodall work on his "sculptured glass."

86 Vase, marquetry with birds and fish

England, 19th century, probably Thomas Webb & Sons
H. 16.7 cm
Museum of Fine Arts, Boston (26.622)

Opaque white on light blue and translucent red and green over colorless glass; marquetry and wheel-cut. Overall design of sea life in water.

This vessel is characteristic of a group of rock crystal-style carved pieces made by Webb & Sons in the oriental style. Although unmarked, it relates closely in color and carving to vases in several private collections stamped Thomas Webb & Sons.

Previously unpublished. For parallels, *English Cameo Glass*, p. 298, C295; p. 383, no. C338.

87 Bottle, *Moore Vase* (classical revival)

Italy, Venice, late 19th century, Compagnia di Venezia e Murano
H. 16.7 cm
Yale University Art Gallery, The Hobart and Edward Small Moore Memorial Collection

Opaque white on frosted deep blue glass; acid-dipped and cameo-carved. Pitted surface, dancing maenad and satyr, bands of ivy, palmettes, and laurel wreath.

For a discussion of the Venetian revival of the cameo tradition see p.

Matheson, Susan, *Ancient Glass in the Yale University Art Gallery*, New Haven: Yale University, 1980, p. 141, no. 47.

88 Vase with classical motifs

Italy, Venice, 1878, possibly Compagnia Venezia e Murano
H. 12.2 cm
Collection of Dr. and Mrs. Leonard S. Rakow

Opaque white over frosted blue glass, acid-dipped and cameo-carved, unfinished.

On either side of a central seahorse, a winged boy holds (rides) a dragon. The vessel does not have the weathered appearance of other Venetian cameo glasses.

Revi, *Nineteenth Century Glass*, pp. 170-172, illus. p. 172; *European Art Glass*, p. 227, fig. 409.

89 Amphora (classical revival)

Italy, Venice, late 19th century

H. 18.9 cm
The Toledo Museum of Art, Gift of Edward
Drummond Libbey, 1923

Opaque white over frosted deep blue glass;
acid-dipped and cameo-carved. Form reconstructed from several large fragments. Handles
carved as satyr masks, ivy around neck, central
motif of a dancing satyr.

For a discussion of the Venetian revival of the
cameo tradition see p.15.

90 Oil lamp

England, Stourbridge, about 1880, probably Thomas Webb & Sons

H. 50.9 cm
Collection of Dr. and Mrs. Leonard S. Rakow

Opaque white over frosted colorless on flashed
red glass; acid-dipped and cameo-carved.

Overall floral and geometric patterns, chimney
of colorless glass with interior frosted red flashing. Silver collar stamped "HINKS & SON'S/
PATENT"; wick holder stamped "Hinks &
Son Patent"; opaque white glass inset on handle
impressed "HINKS'S/DUPLEX/PATENT."

91 Small lamp

England, Wordsley, about 1885, proba-bly Stevens & Williams

H. 20.2 cm
Collection of Dr. and Mrs. Leonard S. Rakow

Opaque white over frosted light blue on
opaque white glass; acid-dipped and cameo-
carved.

Miniature lamp with daisy-like flower on body,
white trumpet flowers on shade and a clear
glass chimney. Three frosted colorless feet.
Brass burner, handle stamped "Albion Lamp
C° • Birmingham •."

Similar lamps appear in the Stevens & Williams design and price books.

92 Apple vase

England, Stourbridge, about 1880; attributed to Thomas Webb & Sons

H. 15.1 cm
Collection of Dr. and Mrs. Leonard S. Rakow

Opaque white over frosted light blue glass;
acid-dipped and cameo-carved. Overall thorn-
apple decoration.

The curved handle is attached only at the top;
three heart-shaped cutouts on the sides.

93 Dolphin scent bottle

England, Amblecote, about 1885; attributed to Thomas Webb & Sons

H. 12.7 cm
Collection of Dr. and Mrs. Leonard S. Rakow

White opal over frosted red glass; acid-dipped
and cameo-carved. Dolphin with silver tail as
the stopper. Carved on base "R<u>d</u> 18109," hallmarks.

94 Claret jug or decanter

England, Stourbridge, about 1884; attributed to Stevens & Williams, possi-bly Joshua Hodgetts

H. 26.2 cm
Collection of Dr. and Mrs. Leonard S. Rakow;
Ex coll. S. Bulgari, Rome

Opaque white over frosted colorless on flashed
red-orange glass; acid-dipped and cameo-
carved.

Bird on a branch pursuing a bee; dragonfly and
butterfly on other side. Handle, mounts, and
masked spout of silver; hallmarks.

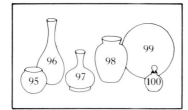

95 Bowl, daisies and clematis

England, Amblecote, about 1880; base impressed "Thomas Webb & Sons"

H. 8.5 cm
Collection of Dr. and Mrs. Leonard S. Rakow

White opal over translucent dark blue on frosted light blue glass; acid-dipped and cameo-carved.

96 Vase, marine decoration

England, Stourbridge, about 1880, possibly George Woodall

H. 24.8 cm
Collection of Dr. and Mrs. Leonard S. Rakow

Opaque white over frosted colorless on a thin layer of yellow-green glass; acid-dipped and cameo-carved.

Long slender neck and bulbous body decorated with shells, seaweed, and coral. A bowl done by Woodall in the Pilkington Museum has similar decoration.

Savage, George, *Glass and Glassware*, London: Octopus Books Limited, 1973, p. 122, for a related bowl.

97 Vase with clematis and leaves

England, Stourbridge, about 1880

H. 14.6 cm
Collection of Dr. and Mrs. Leonard S. Rakow

White opal over transparent red on colorless on opaque flashed yellow on opaque white glass; acid-dipped and cameo-carved. Silver base ring.

98 Vase

England, Wordsley, late 19th century, probably Northwood factory

H. 17.2 cm
Collection of Dr. and Mrs. Leonard S. Rakow

Opaque white over frosted colorless on flashed pink glass; acid-dipped and cameo-carved.

Overall stylized rosette design with three flowers—pansy, tulip, and rose—in oval medallions.

99 Plate, peach branch with bees

England, Stourbridge, about 1890; attributed to Thomas Webb & Sons

D. 21.8 cm
Collection of Dr. and Mrs. Leonard S. Rakow

Opaque white over frosted colorless on flashed red glass; acid-dipped and cameo-carved.

Stylized rosette border; this plate is one of a series, each with a different fruit.

100 Scent or cologne bottle, dahlia design

England, Amblecote, about 1880; attributed to Thomas Webb & Sons

H. 9.8 cm
Collection of Dr. and Mrs. Leonard S. Rakow

White opaque over frosted medium blue glass; acid-dipped and cameo-carved. Overall dahlia design, meander pattern around neck, scroll border at base, and matching stopper. Paper label on base, "Phillips & Pearce/London/155, New Bond Street."

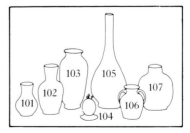

101 Vase, peacock feather

England, Stourbridge, late 19th century, attributed to Thomas Webb & Sons

H. 10.9 cm
Collection of Drs. Jerome and Arline Rosen

Opaque white over frosted medium blue glass; acid-dipped and cameo-carved.

The motif is typical of the flowing Art Nouveau style; the polished eye of the feather contrasts with the satin finish of the body.

102 Vase, gooseberry design

England, Stourbridge, about 1880; attributed to Joshua Hodgetts, Stevens & Williams
H. 16.5 cm
Collection of Dr. and Mrs. Leonard S. Rakow

Opaque white over thick frosted colorless on red flashed glass; acid-dipped and cameo-carved.

Joshua Hodgetts was noted for his carvings of fruits and flowers; he might have executed this excellent carving.

103 Vase, five-layered

England, Amblecote, about 1880; attributed to Thomas Webb & Sons
H. 20.5 cm
Collection of Dr. and Mrs. Leonard S. Rakow

Opaque white over red on colorless on flashed opaque yellow on opaque white glass; acid-dipped and cameo-carved.

Moorish decoration of stylized flowers and leaves carved in the white and red layers.

104 Place card holder

England, Stourbridge, late 19th century; attributed to Thomas Webb & Sons
H. 7.5 cm
Courtesy of Leo Kaplan Antiques

Opaque white over frosted red glass; acid-dipped and cameo-carved. Floral spray within an oval plaque mounted in a gilt bronze frame on a bell-shaped base of cameo glass.

English Cameo Glass, pl. C24.

105 Vase, flowers and butterflies

England, Stourbridge, about 1880, probably Thomas Webb & Sons
H. 34 cm
Collection of Dr. and Mrs. Leonard S. Rakow

Opaque white over thick frosted colorless on flashed light blue glass; acid-dipped and cameo-carved. Decorated with fuschia and other flowers, butterflies on reverse.

106 Two-handled vase

England, Stourbridge, about 1880, probably Stevens & Williams
H. 10.5 cm
Collection of Dr. and Mrs. Leonard S. Rakow

Opaque white over frosted yellow-brown glass; acid-dipped and cameo-carved. Vase in the shape of a miniature Portland Vase (Fig. 5) decorated with a classical rustic shrine; lamp stand and vase on one side, an overgrown rocky outcropping on the other side; wheel-cut rosette on base.

107 Vase, cockerel and floral designs

England, Stourbridge, late 19th century; attributed to Thomas Webb & Sons
H. 15.2 cm
Collection of Dr. and Mrs. Ronald Berg

Opaque white over frosted yellow glass; acid-dipped and cameo-carved. Cockerel in an elaborate medallion on one side and a floral spray within a similar medallion on the other, the background decorated with carved spirals overall.

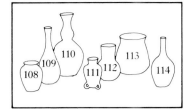

108 Vase, hawthorne or plum blossom and chrysanthemum design

England, Stourbridge, about 1880; attributed to Thomas Webb & Sons

H. 13.1 cm
Collection of Dr. and Mrs. Leonard S. Rakow

Opaque white over frosted light blue glass; acid-dipped and cameo-carved.

Both floral patterns reflect an Oriental influence on English cameo glass. A dragonfly and bee are worked into the design.

109 Vase, wild rose design

England, late 19th century, probably Thomas Webb & Sons

H. 26.3 cm
Courtesy of Leo Kaplan Antiques

Opaque white over red over frosted yellow glass; acid-dipped and cameo-carved. Elaborate overall wild rose pattern.

One of a pair.

110 Vase, double gourd shape

England, late 19th century, probably Thomas Webb & Sons

H. 30.8 cm
Courtesy of Leo Kaplan Antiques

Opaque white over frosted colorless on flashed amethyst glass; acid-dipped and cameo-carved. Wide collar band decorated with oriental-style motifs, overall pattern of gooseberries and bees.

A wonderful example of modeled leaves and berries. A small oval piece of opaque white, deep in the colorless layer, has been fashioned into the body of a small butterfly; the wings and head are carved in relief on the colorless layer.

111 Vase with frosted feet

England, Stourbridge, about 1885, Stevens & Williams

H. 13.9 cm
Collection of Dr. and Mrs. Leonard S. Rakow

Opaque white over colorless on flashed pale yellow-green glass; acid-dipped and cameo-carved. Egg-shaped with a short flared neck decorated with sprays of morning glories and other flowers, rope border at neck and rim. Vase rests on three frosted colorless glass feet.

112 Vase, floral and geometric design

England, Amblecote, about 1880; base impressed "Thomas Webb & Sons"

H. 16.9 cm
Collection of Dr. and Mrs. Leonard S. Rakow

Frosted red over colorless on opaque flashed yellow on opaque white glass; acid-dipped and cameo-carved.

European Art Glass, p. 43, fig. 26.

113 Vase, with stylized flowers

England, Amblecote, about 1877, John Northwood, unsigned

H. 18.5 cm
Collection of Dr. and Mrs. Leonard S. Rakow

Opaque white over frosted pale blue glass; acid-dipped and cameo-carved. Note the delicate overall background scrollwork design. Wheel-cut base design of a six-pointed star in a series of concentric circles with sharp radiating flutes.

John Northwood, illus. on p. 57.

114 Vase, blackberry design

England, Stourbridge, late 19th century, base impressed "Thomas Webb & Sons/Cameo"

H. 22.6 cm
Courtesy of Leo Kaplan Antiques

Opaque white over frosted colorless on flashed amethyst glass; acid-dipped and cameo-carved. Elaborate overall acid-cut geometric and floral background pattern.

Ground pattern is far more complicated than network and rosette fill pattern found on the *rainbow-cased* vase (No. 140).

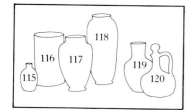

115 Vase

Possibly United States or European, about 1900; base acid-resist "CAMEO"
H. 12.6 cm
Collection of Dr. and Mrs. Leonard S. Rakow

Opaque white over frosted green glass; acid-dipped and cameo-carved. Morning glory vine with flower and leaves.

The green color is unusual in English cameo glass. The vase is either of American or Continental origin, possibly a German attempt at cameo glass carving.

116 Vase, with palm fronds

England, Amblecote, about 1880; base impressed "Thomas Webb & Sons + Cameo + "
H. 29.1 cm
Collection of Dr. and Mrs. Leonard S. Rakow

Opaque white over frosted colorless glass; acid-dipped and cameo-carved. Palm fronds with butterfly on the reverse. White on frosted is an unusual combination.

117 Vase, floral design

England, Amblecote, about 1880; base impressed "Thomas Webb & Sons/ Cameo"
H. 24.9 cm
Collection of Dr. and Mrs. Leonard S. Rakow

Opaque white over translucent red on frosted colorless glass; acid-dipped and cameo-carved.

118 Vase, peacock feathers and butterflies

England, Stourbridge, about 1895; attributed to Thomas Webb & Sons
H. 33.2 cm
Courtesy of Leo Kaplan Antiques

Opaque white over frosted yellow-brown glass; acid-dipped and cameo-carved. Large spray of peacock feathers in a folded embroidered doily, butterflies, all within geometric borders.

This vase combines the subject and style of an Art Nouveau design within a Victorian neo-classical form. Note that the fronds overlap the formal border.

119 Vase, with clematis and butterfly

England, Amblecote, about 1880; base impressed "Thomas Webb & Sons/ Cameo"
H. 22.6 cm
Collection of Dr. and Mrs. Leonard S. Rakow

Opaque white over translucent deep blue on frosted colorless glass; acid-dipped and cameo-carved.

Although this impressed piece by Thomas Webb & Sons has a butterfly in the decoration, not all pieces decorated with a butterfly were made by that company.

120 Decanter with stopper, Rock Crystal style with marquetry panels

England, Stourbridge, about 1880; attributed to Joshua Hodgetts
H. 23.9 cm
Collection of Dr. and Mrs. Leonard S. Rakow

Colorless glass, panels of opaque white on transparent red glass; blown, marquetry technique, cut and carved. Central panel of roses and spider in a web; second cameo strip under handle carved with a floral spray. The decanter and stopper are certainly cut and faceted with stone wheels, but some copper-wheel highlights may have been added. The handle was probably applied hot over the marquetry strip *before* any carving was started. Base numbered 1745.

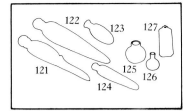

121 Scent bottle, duck's head

England, Amblecote, about 1885
L. 23.7 cm
Collection of Dr. and Mrs. Leonard S. Rakow

Opaque white over frosted brown glass; acid-dipped and cameo-carved. Silver cap stamped with hallmarks of 1885, number in cameo on underside R^d 11109.

This shape was made in red, blue, green, and yellow and in many sizes. Related bottles were made in the shape of swan and falcon heads. According to a letter from Frederick Carder, he made a falcon bottle. There are a few bottles known to be signed by George Woodall, one made for his daughter, Alice.

122 Scent bottle, parrot design

England, Stourbridge, about 1885; attributed to Joshua Hodgetts
L. 25.5 cm
Collection of Dr. and Mrs. Leonard S. Rakow

Opaque white over frosted red glass; acid-dipped and cameo-carved. Tapered form decorated with parrot and butterfly among ferns. Silver top with hallmark, dated 1885. This type of scent bottle was usually held in a silver ring stand with a flat base.

123 Scent bottle with stylized leaf and floral design

England, Stourbridge, about 1880
H. 10.1 cm
Collection of Dr. and Mrs. Leonard S. Rakow

Opaque white over frosted light blue glass; acid-dipped and cameo-carved, elongated flattened egg shape.

The mounting and stopper are silver gilt or gold; hallmark.

124 Scent bottle, bamboo pattern

England, Amblecote, about 1884; attributed to Thomas Webb & Sons
L. 14 cm
Collection of Dr. and Mrs. Leonard S. Rakow

Opaque white over frosted colorless on flashed red glass; acid-dipped and cameo-carved. Tapered flask is carved with an overall bamboo pattern; silver gilt top stamped with hallmark of 1884; number in cameo at tip, R^d 12759

125 Vase, miniature with morning glory and bee pattern

England, Stourbridge, about 1880; attributed to Thomas Webb & Sons
H. 5.4 cm
Collection of Dr. and Mrs. Leonard S. Rakow

Opaque white over transparent red-orange on colorless on yellow green on opaque white glass; acid-dipped and cameo-carved.

126 Miniature vase, plum blossoms

England, Stourbridge, about 1885; attributed to Thomas Webb & Sons
H. 4.9 cm
Collection of Dr. and Mrs. Leonard S. Rakow

Opaque white over frosted colorless on flashed deep red on opaque white glass; acid-dipped and cameo-carved.

127 Jar with silver lid

England, Amblecote; about 1905; attributed to Thomas Webb & Sons
H. 9.1 cm
Collection of Dr. and Mrs. Leonard S. Rakow

Opaque white over frosted light blue glass; acid-dipped and cameo-carved.

Floral pattern; silver ring and hinged top stamped with hallmarks, 1905. This is a good example of the "commercial" cameo glass manufactured at the turn of the century.

The blank was given to Kenneth Northwood by his father; Kenneth Northwood presented it to the Rakows in 1981. This is the same cased and flashed sequence as John Northwood II's *Aphrodite and Attendants* (No. 43).

152 Blank for a Portland Vase

England, 1878, Wordsley, Hodgetts, Richardson and Co.

H. 24.9 cm
Collection of Dr. and Mrs. Leonard S. Rakow

White opal on transparent deep blue glass; blown and cased; the fortieth and last blank made for Joseph Locke. His copy of the Portland (No. 47) was the thirty-ninth.

Corning, *English Cameo Exhibition*, no. 4, p. 23.

153 Unfinished plaque, *Antony and Cleopatra*

England, Amblecote, about 1895

H. 47.7 cm
Collection of Dr. and Mrs. Leonard S. Rakow

Opaque white over transparent brownish purple glass; acid-dipped. Unfinished, flaw in upper right side. The plate has been dipped at least six times to form the design.

George Woodall later completed several Antony and Cleopatra plaques of a slightly different design. One plaque was finished in 1897.

Beard, *Cameo Glass*, p. 118, pl. 12, fig. 45.

154 Vase, *Solitude*

England, probably Wordsley, 1918; base signed "Solitude/1918/J. B. Hill."

H. 10.9 cm
Collection of Dr. and Mrs. Leonard S. Rakow;
Ex coll: James T. Hill, Jr.

White opaque over colorless on a red flashed glass; acid-dipped, cameo-carved, and unfinished. Woodland scene, signed through acid resist; large crack from base through the body.

Revi, *Nineteenth Century Glass*, pp. 142, 145.

155 Carving tool

England, early 20th century

L. 9.2 cm
Collection of Dr. and Mrs. Leonard S. Rakow;
Ex coll: Thomas Webb & Sons

Steel rod inserted in wooden shaft. This tool originally belonged to George Woodall.

156 Tool

England, Stourbridge, early 20th century

L. 13 cm
The Corning Museum of Glass (55.7.1)

Brass tool with steel point in adjustable jaws.

This is the tool frequently illustrated in the photograph which shows Carder carving his *Immortality of the Arts* (No. 49).

Frederick Carder, Ill. 16.

157 Vase, unfinished

England, Stourbridge, 1932, by Joshua Hodgetts

H. 46.5 cm
The Corning Museum of Glass (69.2.2)

Opaque yellow over opaque white on deep blue glass; cameo-carved, unfinished.

A design of flowers and a large rooster has been roughed out, but the piece does not seem to have been acid-dipped.

158 Vase, unfinished

England, late 19th century

H. 22.9 cm
Collection of Dr. and Mrs. Leonard S. Rakow

Opaque white over frosted deep blue glass; acid-dipped and cameo-carved, unfinished.

The unfinished carving depicts Nereids with tridents riding on hippocamps. Roughly carved tritons (?) lift objects over their heads. Although the shape appears to relate to an English form, the glass itself and the motifs are not unlike the small "Venetian" cameo vase (No. 88).

Glossary

Amphoriskos: (a small *amphora*) A small cosmetic flask usually with inverted piriform body, long neck, and two handles. A miniature variation of the large ceramic vessels used to store and transport wine in the classical world.

Annealing: The process of cooling a completed object in an auxiliary part of the glass furnace or a separate furnace (lehr) so that any strain created in the glass during the forming process may be released.

Blank: Any cooled glass object which requires further forming or decoration to be finished.

Cage Cup: (See *Diatretum*)

Cameo Glass: Glass of one color cased or covered with one or more layers of contrasting color. These outer layers are carved in relief by various techniques to produce a design which stands out from the background.

Cased Glass: Glass of one color covered with a glass of another color thick enough (more than 1 mm) to be cut or carved with decorative motifs.

Carving: The decorative technique whereby glass is removed from an object's surface by various hand-held tools such as files, points, graving instruments, or riffles. The term is general and is somewhat misleading since the glass is actually chipped, abraded, or spalled by these implements and not carved in the sense of wood or meat.

Core-forming: The technique of forming a vessel by trailing molten glass over a core supported by a metal rod. The glass was probably applied with another metal rod. The object was removed from the rod and annealed. After annealing, the core was scraped out.

Cutting: The decorative technique whereby glass is ground away from an object's surface by a rotating stone wheel fed with water. See "engraving" and "carving."

Diatretum (cage cup): (Latin) A vessel decorated by undercutting so that the surface decoration stands free of the body of the glass, supported only by struts or pins, giving the appearance of an openwork cage.

Diatretarius: (Latin) A craftsman who finished or decorated glass vessels by abrasive techniques such as cutting, engraving, or carving.

Engraving: The technique of cutting into the surface of a glass by holding it against a rotating copper wheel fed with abrasive. See "cutting" and "carving."

Flashing: The application of a very thin (less than 1 mm) layer of one color over a contrasting color. This layer is too thin to be worked in relief. The term is often (and incorrectly) used to describe cased glass.

Gather: (see Paraison)

Glass: A homogeneous material which has a random, liquid-like (non-crystalline) molecular structure. The manufacturing process for glass requires that the raw materials be heated to react chemically so as to form a completely fused melt which is then cooled rapidly so that it becomes rigid without crystallizing.

Hookah: (Arabic) A water pipe used throughout the Near East and East.

Inlay: Any object fastened into the surface of a larger object and cemented into place as part of a decorative pattern. Note: Glass inlays may range from simple square monochrome tiles to complicated mosaic glass elements.

Intaglio: (Italian) A method of engraving by which the decoration is cut into the material and lies beneath the surface plane.

Lathe-cut: The technique whereby blanks of glass in the general shape of an object are mounted and turned slowly with the aid of a bow or handled wheel while a tool (probably of metal or wood) fed with an abrasive is held against the glass in order to cut sharp profiles or to polish the overall surface.

Lehr: See annealing.

Marquetry (*marqueterie de verre*): The decorative technique of applying hot elements of glass onto a vessel and marvering them into the surface. These elements are often further elaborated by cutting, engraving, or carving. The term "padding" also has been used to describe hot glass trails or pads which are applied to a vessel.

Marvering: Rolling softened glass over a flat surface in order to smooth out the vessel wall or consolidate trail decoration applied to the object.

Mold-pressing: Forcing or pressing hot glass into an open or multi-part mold. In antiquity, the molten glass was probably pressed with a metal or wooden implement.

Overlay: See cased glass. Note: This term is often used to describe both flashed and cased glass.

Paraison: A gather of glass, at the end of a blowpipe, which has already been slightly inflated with a small bubble of air.

***Pâte-de-verre*:** (French) A glass made by fusing powdered glass in a mold.

Resist: A preparation of wax, gum, paint, or paper applied to the glass surface to protect it from the etching effect of hydroflouric acid or sandblasting.

Sandblasting: Abrasives directed under high pressure against a glass surface in order to remove the unprotected (see "resist") areas and create designs. Note: Several specialized nozzles have been developed to permit fast removal of the outer layer or a stipple effect by the use of a controlled jet releasing one abrasive particle at a time.

Skyphos: (Greek) A footed cup usually with ovoid body and two vertical handles.

Stained Glass: Glass which has been covered with a metallic oxide and reheated to cause a coloring of the surface. The term is often (and incorrectly) used to describe flashed glass.

Strain Cracks: The small and irregular fissures which occur in the body of a vessel and resemble similar cracks in ice. These are caused by internal stress, a result of inadequate annealing or sudden accidental thermal shocks.

***Vitriarius*:** (Latin) The craftsman who worked glass when it was hot by techniques such as blowing, casting, or core-forming.

Weathering: The result of interaction between the surface of a glass and its environment, usually the result of chemical attack whether by water or air. Note: The degree or lack of weathering depends upon the chemical composition of the glass itself, its thermal history, and the chemical nature of its environment.

AJA—American Journal of Archaeology

Arts of Islam
Hayward Gallery. *The Arts of Islam*. April 8 - July 4, 1976. London: The Arts Council of Great Britain, 1976.

Beard, *Antiques*
Beard, Geoffrey W. "English Makers of Cameo Glass." *Antiques* 65, no. 6, June 1954, pp. 472-474.

Beard, *Nineteenth Century Glass*
Beard, Geoffrey W. *Nineteenth Century Cameo Glass*. Newport, England: Ceramic Book Co., 1956.

Bushell
Bushell, Stephen W., *Chinese Art*, 2nd ed. Victoria and Albert Museum, London: His Majesty's Stationery Office, 1919. 2 vols.

Charleston, *Masterpieces*
Charleston, Robert J. *Masterpieces of Glass, A World History from The Corning Museum of Glass*. New York: Harry N. Abrams, Inc., 1980. (A Corning Museum of Glass Monograph).

Cooney, *Egyptian Cat.*
Cooney, John D. *Catalogue of Egyptian Antiquities in The British Museum IV, Glass*. London: The Trustees of the British Museum, British Publications Ltd., 1976.

Corning, *English Cameo Exhibition*
Corning Museum of Glass. *English Nineteenth Century Cameo Glass*. Corning, New York: Corning Museum of Glass, 1963.

Davids Samling
Davids Samling, Islamisk Kunst, Copenhagen, 1975.

Davidson, *English Cameo*
Davidson, Ruth. "Special Events: English Cameo Glass." *Antiques* 83, no. 6, June 1963, p. 694.

Davidson, *Masterpiece*
Davidson, Ruth. "A Nineteenth-century Masterpiece in Cameo Glass." *Antiques* 28, no. 1, July 1935, p. 6.

Dudley
Dudley Art Gallery. *English "Rock Crystal" Glass 1875-1925*. Dudley, England: Dudley Art Gallery, 1976.

Duffy
Duffy, E. Mary. "Philip Pargeter and John Northwood I, Cameo Glass Pioneers." *Antiques* 82, no. 6, Dec. 1962, pp. 639-641.

Eisen
Eisen, Gustavus A., assisted by Fahim Kouchakji. *Glass*. New York: William E. Rudge, 1927. 2 vols.

Eisen, *Antiques*
Eisen, Gustavus A. "The Place and Meaning of the Portland Vase." *Antiques* 16, no. 1, 1929, pp. 105-108.

English Cameo Glass
Grover, Ray and Lee. *English Cameo Glass*. New York: Crown Publishers, Inc., 1980.

European Art
Grover, Ray and Lee. *Carved and Decorated European Art Glass*. Rutland, Vermont: Charles E. Tuttle Company, 1970.

Farrar
Farrar, Estelle Sinclaire. "John Northwood and English Cameo Glass." *Arts & Antiques* 4, Issue 4, July/Aug. 1981, pp. 50-55.

Gaines, Edith, "Portraits"
"Collector's Notes: Cameo-Glass Portraits—A First." *Antiques* 109, no. 6, June 1976, p. 1171.

Gardner, *Frederick Carder*
Gardner, Paul V. *The Glass of Frederick Carder.* New York: Crown Publishers, Inc., 1971.

Goldstein, *Pre-Roman*
Goldstein, Sidney M. *Roman and Pre-Roman Glass in The Corning Museum of Glass.* Corning, New York: The Corning Museum of Glass, 1979.

Gréau Cat.
Froehner, Wilhelm. *Collection Julien Gréau, Verrerie antique, Émaillerie et Poterie, appartenant à M. John Pierpont Morgan,* Paris: s.n., 1903. 6 vols.

Guide
The Corning Museum of Glass. *Glass from The Corning Museum of Glass, A Guide to the Collections.* Corning: The Corning Museum of Glass, 1955 (rev. 1958, 1965, 1974).

Guttery, *Broad-Glass*
Guttery, D.R. *From Broad-Glass to Cut Crystal.* London: Leonard Hill, 1956.

Harden, *Ancient Glass, II: Roman*
Harden, Donald B. "Ancient Glass, II: Roman." *The Archaeological Journal* 126, 1970, pp. 44-77.

Haynes
D.E.L. Haynes. *The Portland Vase.* 2nd ed., rev. London: The Trustees of the British Museum, British Museum Publications, 1975.

Hind, "Portland Vase"
Hind, John G.F. "Greek and Roman Epic Scenes on the Portland Vase." *JHS* 99, 1979, pp. 20-25.

Honey
Honey, William B. *Glass: A Handbook and a Guide to the Museum Collections, Victoria and Albert Museum.* London: Ministry of Education, 1946.

JGS—Journal of Glass Studies

JHS—The Journal of Hellenic Studies

Kisa
Kisa, Anton. *Das Glas im Altertume.* Leipzig: K.W. Hiersemann, 1908. 3 vols.

Kunstmuseum Luzern
Kunstmuseum Luzern. *3000 Jahre Glaskunst von Antike bis zum Jugendstil.* Luzern: Mengis + Sticher AG, 1981.

Lamm, *Mitt. Gläser*
Lamm, Carl J. *Mittelalterliche Gläser und Steinschnittarbeiten aus dem Nahen Osten.* Berlin: Dietrich Reimer, 1929 and 1930. 2 vols.

Lamm, *Samarra*
Lamm, Carl J. *Das Glas von Samarra.* Berlin: Dietrich Reimer, 1928.

London. Science Museum
Descriptive Catalogue of the Collection Illustrating Glass Technology by S.E. Jason. London: HMSO, 1969.

Lucas, *Materials*, 1962
Lucas, Alfred. *Ancient Egyptian Materials and Industries.* Rev. J.R. Harris, 4th ed. London: E. Arnold, 1962.

Masterpieces
Harden, D.B.; Painter, K.S.; Pinder-Wilson, R.H.; Tait, Hugh. *Masterpieces of Glass.* London: Trustees of The British Museum, 1968.

Moss, *Glass Snuff Bottles*
Moss, Hugh M. *Glass Snuff Bottles from China from the Mayer Collection.* Exhibition, Steuben Glass, Sept. 9-Oct. 3, 1980. New York: Color Xerox Catalog, u. p.

Moss, *Snuff Bottles*
Moss, Hugh M. *Snuff Bottles of China.* London: Bibelot Publishers Ltd., 1971.

John Northwood
Northwood, John II. *John Northwood, His Contribution to the Stourbridge Flint Glass Industry, 1850-1902*. Stourbridge, England: Mark and Moody, 1958.

Northwood, *J. Soc. Glass Tech 33*
Northwood, John II. "Stourbridge Cameo Glass." News and Reviews, *Journal of the Society of Glass Technology* 33, 1949, pp. 106-113.

Nyman, B.
Nyman, B. *Illustrated Catalogue in Two Volumes of the Nyman Collection of Cameo Glass, Porcelain Enamelling and Pâte-sur-pâte*. Vol. I-Cameo Glass and Porcelain Enamelling. [London: Herbert Hurst & Co., 1957].

Oliver, *JGS 3*
Oliver, Prudence. "Islamic Relief Cut Glass: A Suggested Chronology." *JGS* 3, 1961, pp. 9-29.

Plesch, "Chinese Glass"
Plesch, Peter H. "Some Approaches to the Study of Later Chinese Glass," in *Festschrift für Peter Wilhelm Meister* by Annaliese Ohm and Horst Reber, ed. Hamburg: Dr. Ernst Hanswedell & Co., 1975, pp 71-79.

Reilly and Savage
Reilly, Robin and Savage, George. *Wedgewood, The Portrait Medallions*. London: Barrie and Jenkins, 1974.

Revi, *Nineteenth Century Glass*
Revi, Albert C. *Nineteenth Century Glass, Its Genesis and Development*. New York: Thomas Nelson and Sons, 1967.

Short History
Zerwick, Chloe. *A Short History of Glass*. Corning: The Corning Museum of Glass, 1980.

Simon, *Portlandvase*
Simon, Erika. *Die Portlandvase*. Mainz: Verlag des Römisch-Germanischen Zentralmuseums, 1957.

Smith Cat.
The Corning Museum of Glass. *Glass from the Ancient World: The Ray Winfield Smith Collection, A Special Exhibition*. Corning: The Corning Museum of Glass, 1957.

Toledo, *Ancient Glass*
Riefstahl, Rudolf M. *Ancient and Near Eastern Glass*. Toledo: The Toledo Museum of Art, 1961.

Turner, *J. Soc. Glass Tech. 8*
Turner, W.E.S., "Noteworthy Productions of the Glass Craftsman's Art, II. Mr. John Northwood's Plaque of *Aphrodite*." *Journal Society of Glass Technology* 8, 1924, pp. 92T-93T.

Vatican Cat.
Fremersdorf, Fritz. *Antikes, Islamisches und Mittelalterlisches Glas* (Catalogo del Museo Sacro 5). Citta Del Vaticano, 1975.

Wakefield
Wakefield, Hugh. *Nineteenth Century British Glass*. London: Faber and Faber, 1961.

Warren, "Chinese Glass"
Warren, Phelps. "Later Chinese Glass. 1650-1900." *JGS* 19, 1977, pp. 84-126.

Wills
Wills, Geoffrey. "Sir William Hamilton and the Portland Vase." *Apollo* 110, no. 211, Sept. 1979, pp. 195-201.

Woodward, *Art, Feat, and Mystery*
Woodward, H.W. *Art, Feat and Mystery: The Story of Thomas Webb & Sons, Glassmakers*. Stourbridge, England: Mark and Moody, 1978.

Index

A

abrasive powders, 11
acid-cutting, acid-dipped, 48, 56, 111, 129
acid-resist, acid-resist ink, 55
Adam and Eve, 44, 108
aegis, 98
Aeneas, 99
agate, 11
Albion Lamp Co., Birmingham, 119
Alexandria, 99, 101
Amblecote, 50
America, 55-56
amethyst, semi-precious stone, 106
Amon-Re, 99
amphitheater, 104, 105
Amphitrite, 45
amphora, amphoriskos, 101, 119
Andromache, plaque, 115
Andromeda, 43
annealed, annealing, 47, 128
Antony and Cleopatra, plaque, 129
Aphrodite, 99, 103, 110, 128
Aphrodite and Attendants, plaque, 48, 55, 103, 110, 128
Apollo, 129
appliqués, 107, 118, 127
arabesque design, pattern, 114, 125
Ara Pacis, 8
Archaeological Museum, Florence, 14
Archangel Michael, 44, 108
Ariadne, 104
Armenian Girl, The, 52
Art Nouveau, Art Nouveau style, 56, 123, 127
Asiatic Victories, 8
Athena, 98, 99
Augustan peace, Augustan Rome, 9, 98
Augustus, 8, 98
Augustus and Roma, 98
Auldjo Jug, The, 14, 100
Aurora, 45

B

Bain du Diane, Le, 115
Barbe, Jules, 50, 116, 117
basalt, 11
Beijing (Peking), 36
Berg, Dr. and Mrs. Ronald, 125
Bertini, 52, 54
Besançon, Besançon pitcher, 103, 104
Bibliothèque Nationale, Paris, 15
Birmingham Art Gallery, The, 43
Birmingham Museum of Art, 43
Birth of Venus, vase, 111
Bismark, 52
bituminous paint, 53
Black Sea, 98

blank; blanks; blanks, annealed; blank plaque, 6, 9, 10, 44, 49, 53, 112, 128
Blount, Collection of Dr. and Mrs. Henry, 113
Boam, H.J., 49, 112
Bohm, August, 44
Borghese Vase, 15
Boscoreale, 8
Boshan, Boshan (Poshan), 36, 37
Bott, Thomas, 42, 51
Boucher, François, 52, 56, 115
bow drill, 11
Boxing Day Meet, The, plaque, 112
bran pad, bran filled sack, 43, 47
Brill, Robert H., 10, 101
Brierley Hill Glass Works, 46, 47, 53
British Museum, The, London, 6, 13, 14, 30, 44, 99, 100
Broadfield House Glass Museum, Dudley, 48, 49, 110, 112
Brookman, Lord, 114
burnishings, 50

C

Cadman, Dr. and Mrs. Samuel Parkes, 52, 112
Caesar, Julius, 8
cameo-carved, carving, cameo glass carving, 48, 55, 56
cameo tile of Scaurus, 16
Campbell, Dr. G.C., 48
Canova, Antonio, 52, 54, 115
canteen vase, 117
Capri, villa of Tiberius, 102
Carder, Frederick, 49, 50, 108, 111, 121, 123, 128, 129
Carlyle, Thomas, 42
carnelian, 106
carved, carved cameo glass, carver, carving, 11, 49, 54, 55
carving tool, 129
Casa di Goethe, 100
case, cased, cased blank, cased glass, casing, 10, 11, 46, 47, 53, 54, 56
Castellani Medusa head, 16
chalcedony; chalcedony, banded, 11, 98
chalice, 127
chariot of Aphrodite, 102
Chariot Skyphos, 15
Chinese and Japanese glass, 54
Chinese lacquer work, 108
Chinese pattern, Chinese style, 116, 117
Chlamys, 104
Chrysler Museum, Norfolk, Virginia, 30, 49, 105, 107, 112, 114
Clarkes, S., patent trademark, 126
Cleopatra, 116
Cleopatra, plaque, 129
Cleopatra, vase, 116

18 - 835